TRAV
THE

presents the World Premiere of

READER

by ARIEL DORFMAN

Director Ian Brown
Designer Tim Hatley
Composer John Irvine
Lighting Designer Ian Sommerville
Costume Designer Lynn Jeffery
Assistant Director Deborah Yhip

Dugald Bruce-Lockhart
Chris Campbell
Clive Merrison
Hermione Norris
Tanya Ronder
Roger Swaine

First performance at the Traverse Theatre on Friday 28 July 1995

TRAVERSE
THEATRE

Over the last three decades Edinburgh's Traverse Theatre has had a seminal influence on British and international theatre and it continues to be a powerhouse of new writing.

In 1992 the Traverse moved to a new home as imaginative as the work which is presented on it's stage. From it's tiny 100 seat theatre in Edinburgh's Grassmarket, this move was a giant leap into the unknown, but it was a move which proved even more successful than the Traverse could have imagined.

Audiences have doubled. The Traverse has taken full advantage of the increased artistic opportunities and, it's energy and commitment to presenting the very best new work is undimmed.

The Traverse Theatre is funded by the Scottish Arts Council which recognises the Traverse's importance as one of the country's leading theatres for new work; and by Edinburgh District Council which recognises the important contribution which the Traverse makes to the social, cultural and economic life of the City. The Traverse also generates significant support from the business sector for its full and diverse all year round programme.

TRAVERSE
THEATRE

ARIEL DORFMAN was born in Argentina in 1942, but is a Chilean citizen forced into exile after a CIA-backed coup established General Augusto Pinochet as dictator in 1973, ousting the socialist government of Salvador Allende. Dorfman was permitted to return in 1983 but, in 1987 he was arrested and deported. Since democracy returned to his country in 1990, he divides his time between Chile and the United States. He teaches at Duke University, and lives with his wife, Angelica, and their youngest son, Joaquin.

Dorfman is well known for his cultural criticism, *How to Read Donald Duck* (1971). He has also written three novels, a collection of short stories, a book of poems, and most recently his new novel *Konfidenz* . His plays include *Widows* (with Tony Kushner), *Reader* and the much acclaimed *Death and the Maiden*, which won the Olivier Award for Best Play in London and was adapted for film by the author and directed by Roman Polanski. With his eldest son, Rodrigo, he recently wrote the BBC teleplay, *Prisoners In Time*, starring John Hurt. He has been called the "*conscience of the New World Order*" and "*a world novelist of the first category.*" (Washington Post)

Ariel Dorfman is obsessed with giving a voice to those who cannot speak; the dead, the missing, those whose lives are interrupted by history. Like many of his characters, Dorfman's own life was interrupted by his many exiles and although grounded in Chile, he addresses all diasporic communities, exploring life on the frontier, a fluctuating space between past and present, the physical and the psychic.

"*For many years I have been struggling with a problem that many exiles have: How are you faithful to your country while, in fact, you are writing for people who have not been your fellow countrymen for a long time? The experience of inventing that faraway country, Chile, has been central to everything I've done, keeping it alive. And yet, there is a sense that though it is Chile, it is not a local Chile, it's a Chile of the imagination, a Chile of the mind. I believe strongly that if there is salvation, if such a word exists or has a meaning, it's in that capacity to create an imaginary world which gives an alternative meaning to the fate that has been imposed upon us.*"

(Jenifer Berman interview with Ariel Dorfman for BOMB magazine)

TRAVERSE
THEATRE

Time: The Future
Place: Everywhere

Nick Lucas / Enrique Morales / David Malko	**Dugald Bruce-Lockhart**
Man	**Christopher Campbell**
Daniel Lucas / Don Alfonso Morales	**Clive Merrison**
Irene / Jacqueline	**Hermione Norris**
Tanya / Sonia	**Tanya Ronder**
The Director	**Roger Swaine**
Stage Manager	**Gavin Johnson**
Deputy Stage Manager	**Heather Wilson**
Assistant Stage Manager	**Penny Thompson**
Wardrobe Supervisor	**Lynn Jeffery**
Cutter	**Jackie Holt**
Wardrobe Assistant	**Karen Smith**

IAN BROWN is Artistic Director of the Traverse Theatre. Productions for the Traverse include: MOSCOW STATIONS (Traverse & Garrick); UNIDENTIFIED HUMAN REMAINS, POOR SUPER MAN (Traverse & Hampstead); ANNA - AN OPERA, THE HOUSE AMONG THE STARS, COLUMBUS, THE BENCH, THE COW JUMPED OVER THE MOON, PIGPLAY, HARDIE & BAIRD, TALLY'S BLOOD, THE HOPE SLIDE, INES DE CASTRO, A LIGHT IN THE VILLAGE, LOOSE ENDS, AWAY, THE COLLECTION (Traverse); HANGING THE PRESIDENT (Traverse & BAC); BONDAGERS (Traverse & Tramway); Ian was formerly Artistic Director of TAG Theatre Company and before that Associate Director of the Theatre Royal, Statford East.

DUGALD BRUCE-LOCKHART *(Nick/Enrique/David)*: Trained at RADA. Theatre work includes: THE WOOD DEMON, BLOODY POETRY, OUR COUNTRY'S GOOD, MYSTERY PLAYS (RADA); HENRY V1: BATTLE FOR THE THRONE (RSC Stratford & World Tour); A STREETCAR NAMED DESIRE, ENTERTAINING MR SLOANE (Byre Theatre).

CHRISTOPHER CAMPBELL *(Man)*: Theatre work includes: MOUNTAIN GIANTS, MACBETH, DRAGON, PYGMALION, THE NIGHT OF THE IGUANA, JO-JO THE MELON DONKEY, THE FRANKLINS TALE (Royal National Theatre); WHAT EVERY WOMAN KNOWS (West Yorkshire Playhouse); PURGATORY IN INGOLSTADT, PIONEERS IN INGOLSTADT (The Gate Theatre); TRANSLATIONS, ALL MY SONS (Birmingham Rep); A MIDSUMMER NIGHT'S DREAM (Globe Theatre, Regina, Sask, Canada); LE PERROQUET NOIR (Theatre De Broccoli, Brussels); BLACK ICE, ROBIN HOOD (Derby Playhouse); DR FAUSTUS, CHRISTIE IN LOVE (Vox Touring Theatre); BEAUX' STRATAGEM, AS YOU LIKE IT (English Touring Theatre). TV includes; COASTING, FAMILIES, SHERLOCK HOLMES AND THE MISSING LINK, WORLD IN ACTION, CONFESSIONAL.

TRAVERSE
THEATRE

TIM HATLEY *(Designer)*: Theatre work includes: MOSCOW STATIONS (Traverse & Garrick), POOR SUPERMAN (Traverse & Hampstead); OUT OF A HOUSE WALKED A MAN (Lyttelton Theatre); THE THREE LIVES OF LUCIE CABROL, CINDERELLA, H.M.S. PINAFORE, DIE FLEDERMAUS (National Theatre); THE NOSE (Nottingham Playhouse); RETURN OF ULYSSES (Buxton Festival Opera); LADY FROM THE SEA (Lyric Hamersmith); THE MISUNDERSTANDING, DAMNED FOR DESPAIR (Gate Theatre); RICHARD III (RSC); CHATSKY (Almeida); THE TAMING OF THE SHREW (National Theatre of Athens & Sheffield Crucible). Opera work includes: ORPHEUS IN THE UNDERWORLD (Opera North); IL TRAVATORE (Scottish Opera). Dance work includes: ROUGHCUT (Rambert Dance Co); FLAMING DESIRE (Extemporary Dance Theatre).

JOHN IRVINE *(Composer)*: Theatre work includes: MOSCOW STATIONS (Traverse & Garrick), POOR SUPERMAN, UNIDENTIFIED HUMAN REMAINS (Traverse & Hampstead), EUROPE, THE HOPE SLIDE, BROTHERS OF THUNDER, BUCHANAN, PHASES OF THE MOON, THE LIFE OF STUFF, COLUMBUS: BLOODING THE OCEAN, THE STRUGGLE OF THE DOGS AND THE BLACK (Traverse); TRAINSPOTTING (Citizens' & Bush Theatre); THE NEW MENOZA (Gate Theatre); RUNNING WITH MY HEAD DOWN (Into The Blue); WHALE (Cumbernauld); THE BABY (RSAMD). Film work includes: DOG DAYS.

LYNN JEFFERY *(Costume Designer)*: Lynn has worked for the Traverse for 6 years. Freelance work includes: Test Department, NVA, Mouth Music, Clanjamfre, Cutter at Citizens', London Baroque Opera, Bridge Lane Theatre - Battersea, Harlow Playhouse.

CLIVE MERRISON *(Daniel/Don Alfonso)*: Theatre work includes: THE BROWNING VERSION (Greenwich Theatre); THE MADNESS OF GEORGE THE THIRD (National Theatre & US Tour); THE POPE AND THE WITCH (Comedy Theatre); BASTARD ANGEL, TROILUS AND CRESSIDA, PRINCIPIA SCRIPTORIAE, MUCH ADO ABOUT NOTHING, MOSCOW COLD (RSC); THE POSSESSED (Open Space); ARTAUD AT RODEZ, VAMPIRE, THE LAST RESORT (Bush Theatre); SATURDAY, SUNDAY, MONDAY, THE MISANTHROPE, THE FRONT PAGE (NT at the Old Vic). TV includes: TOMORROW PEOPLE, STALIN, PIE IN THE SKY, CARIANI AND THE COURTESAN, FREUD, PRIVATE SCHULTZ, THE GLITTERING PRIZES, REILLY ACE OF SPIES, SHINE ON HARVEY MOON, KIT CURRAN RADIO SHOW, A VERY BRITISH COUP. Film work includes: AN AWFULLY BIG ADVENTURE, HEAVENLY CREATURES, COMING OUT OF THE ICE, FIREFOX.

HERMIONE NORRIS *(Irene/Jaqueline)*: Trained at LAMDA. Theatre work includes: CHARLEY'S AUNT, LOOK BACK IN ANGER (Royal Exchange, Manchester); SEPTEMBER TIDE (Comedy Theatre); PYGMALION (National, London); THREE JUDGEMENTS IN ONE (Gate Theatre); MAN AND SUPERMAN (Citizens'); A MIDSUMMER NIGHT'S DREAM, HABEAS CORPUS (Mercury); DAISY PULLS IT OFF (Thorndike). Television work includes: RETURN OF COLUMBUS, POIROT, DROP THE DEAD DONKEY, THE MEN'S ROOM, CASUALTY, BETWEEN THE LINES, UNDER THE HAMMER, BLOOD RIGHTS, THE COUNT OF SOLAR, CLARISSA.

TRAVERSE
THEATRE

TANYA RONDER *(Tanya/Sonia)*: Theatre work includes: UGANDA, THE MADNESS OF ESME AND SHAZ (Royal Court); IF WE SHADOWS (Insomniac Productions); ROSA CARNIVORA (Wink); BURNING EVEREST (West Yorkshire Playhouse); SMIRNOVA'S BIRTHDAY (Arts Threshold); A CURSED PLACE (Grove); MAKING PLAYS WORK (Watford Palace); RESISTIBLE RISE OF ARTURO UI, NAPOLI MILIONARIA (National, London); BLOODY POETRY (London City); JANE EYRE (Derby Playhouse). TV includes: PRIME SUSPECT, THE BILL, CENTRE OF GRAVITY, JUTE CITY, WHAT WE TALK ABOUT WHEN WE TALK ABOUT LOVE, IN SICKNESS AND IN HEALTH, AN ACTOR'S LIFE FOR ME, DOCTOR AT THE TOP, PERFORMACES.

IAN SOMMERVILLE *(Lighting Designer)*:Theatre work includes: MOSCOW STATIONS (Traverse & Garrick), POOR SUPERMAN (Traverse & Hampstead); LOOT (Watford Palace); POOR BEAST IN THE RAIN (Druid Theatre); H.R.H. (Theatr Clwyd). Opera work includes: L'HEURE ESPAGNOL; GIANNI SCHICCHI; THE PEARL FISHERS; THE MARRIAGE OF FIGARO; FIGARO-THE UNTOLD TALE; LADDERS AND SNAKES; YOLANDE (Opera North); THE MIDSUMMER MARRIAGE, DON GIOVANNI (Scottish Opera); KING PRIAM (English National Opera/Flanders Opera/Opera North); TURN OF THE SCREW (Buxton Festival/Pimlico Opera). Set design work includes: TOSCA (Crystal Clear Opera); UN BALLO IN MASCHERA (Opera Nova); POISONED SILENCE (Opera North).

ROGER SWAINE *(The Director)*: Theatre work includes: WHEN WE DEAD AWAKEN, THE TRIALS OF JOAN OF ARC, A MIDSUMMER NIGHTS DREAM, DANIEL DERONDA (69 Theatre Company); THE MERCHANT OF VENICE, THE TEMPEST, THE MISER (Royal Exchange, Manchester); PETER PAN (Scala); ERB (Strand); MISTER (Duchess); ONE AT NIGHT (Royal Court); TINA, LAND OF PALMS, SKUNGPOOMERY, THE MEMORANDUM (Orange Tree); ON BORROWED TIME (Southwark Playhouse); AS YOU LIKE IT, THE CAUCASIAN CHALK CIRCLE, PLAYING WITH FIRE, A PENNY FOR A SONG (RSC); RACING DEMON, MURMURING JUDGES, THE ABSENCE OF WAR, JOHNNY ON A SPOT, THE WIND IN THE WILLOWS (Royal National Theatre). TV includes: AS YOU LIKE IT, A CRACK IN THE ICE, WHEN WE DEAD AWAKEN, SHADOW OF THE NOOSE, FRONT PAGE STORY, CROWN COURT, THE BILL, WAITING FOR GOD, DOWN TO EARTH. Radio includes: THE CRUCIBLE, JULIUS CAESAR, EXPEDITION, MIXTURE FOR MURDER, LITTLE RED LINE, DIDO QUEEN OF CARTHAGE, AN UNSPEAKABLE CRIME, AS A MAN GROWS OLDER, THE FORBIDDEN SHORE. Film includes: A DREAM CALLED FORTH. Has also directed over 100 freelance productions both here and abroad.

DEBORAH YHIP *(Assistant Director)*: Deborah has been an Assistant Director for the Traverse since October '93. Her directing experience includes: DOWNFALL (Contact Theatre, Manchester); SOUL SISTERS MELODY (Everyman Theatre, Liverpool); THE HOUSE OF BLUE LEAVES (by John Guare for Central School of Speech & Drama); AIN'T I A WOMAN (Assati Theatre).

TRAVERSE
THEATRE

THE COMPANY

PROPS, COSTUMES & SCENERY BUILT BY TRAVERSE WORKSHOPS

With thanks to:
BLF
Niamh Gallagher - Stage Management Placement
Print Photography by Kevin Low
Production Photography by Sean Hudson
LEVER BROTHERS for Wardrobe Care

TRAVERSE
THEATRE

SPONSORSHIP

BANK OF SCOTLAND
A FRIEND FOR LIFE ·
300 YEARS OF BANKING SERVICE

CORPORATE ASSOCIATE SCHEME

LEVEL ONE

Bell Lawrie White & Co
Clydesdale Bank
Dawson International
Dundas & Wilson CS
KLP Scotland
The Leith Agency
Scottish Brewers
Scottish Equitable plc
Scottish Life Assurance Company
United Distillers

LEVEL TWO

Allingham & Co, Solicitors
Anderson Strathern
Isle of Skye 8 Year Old Blend
Royal Scottish Assurance
The Royal Bank of Scotland
Willis Corroon Scotland Ltd

LEVEL THREE

Alistir Tait FGA Antique & Fine Jewellery
Gibson Kerr & Co WS, Solicitor
Moores Rowland, Chartered Accountants
Nicholas Groves Raines, Architects

Gerrard & Medd, Designers
KPMG
Scottish Post Office Board

With thanks to Navy Blue Design, designers for the Traverse &
to George Stewarts the printers.

The Traverse Theatre's work would not be possible without the support of:

THE SCOTTISH **ARTS** COUNCIL

Traverse Theatre, Cambridge Street, Edinburgh EH1 2ED, 0131 228 1404
Registered Charity No. ED 1964/68

READER

by Ariel Dorfman

The author wishes to recognise Arthur Penn for generously helping to elaborate, over many months, an earlier version of this play. Thanks also to the Mark Taper Forum for a workshop of the text and the Sydney Theatre Company in Australia and Steppenwolf in Chicago for readings of the play. A special appreciation to Ian Brown, for his faith in this project; to Rodrigo, for his comments; and to Angelica, as always, for her suggestions and, above all, her patience.

This play is for Rodrigo and Joaquin,
with thanks for their company and their existence

Cast of Characters

DANIEL LUCAS, *around fifty years old. Could be older. Or a bit younger. The same actor plays* DON ALFONSO MORALES.

IRENE, *a secretary, in her thirties. The same actress plays* JACQUELINE.

NICK (NICHOLAS) LUCAS, *Daniel Lucas's son, around twenty-five/thirty. The same actor plays* ENRIQUE MORALES *and* DAVID MALKO, *a writer.*

DIRECTOR, *around Daniel Lucas's age. Could be a bit older or a bit younger.*

TANYA, *a shadow woman, Daniel Lucas's former wife, between twenty and thirty years old. The same actress plays* SONIA, *David Malko's wife.*

MAN, *ageless. Can only play himself.*

Time: the near future.

Place: everywhere.

The play can be staged without an intermission.

ACT ONE

Darkness.

A beam of light comes up on the MAN *on one side of the stage. He makes a gesture and next to him a chair appears in another beam of light. He examines the chair, measuring it carefully, with some satisfaction. He makes another gesture and the chair disappears, swallowed by the darkness and, simultaneously, swirling, murky lights go up on an office. We can vaguely see the figures of a man and a woman sitting on either side of a desk, but we cannot hear what they are saying. The* MAN *walks up to the lighted area, stops at its edge, listens. Then he begins to measure the perimeter of the office. He smiles. He makes another gesture and the light grows and we begin to hear the man and the woman: he is* DON ALFONSO MORALES *and the woman is his secretary,* JACQUELINE. DON ALFONSO *is a man of some fifty years, though he could be older – or younger: streaks of white in his hair, prominent eyebrows, a suit with a stiff shirt and tie.* JACQUELINE *is an extremely attractive, vivacious woman in her thirties. The office furniture is very sparse: a desk (its top is held in place by two pillars of books), two chairs, a window through which we can see verdant forests. Next to the desk is an umbrella.*

DON ALFONSO. Next!

JACQUELINE. No subsidy at all, Don Alfonso? Not even one peso?

DON ALFONSO. Nothing. No talent. You can't argue with talent. You possess it or you don't. And this lady – no matter what her other attributes –

JACQUELINE. But her husband knows the Minister of –

DON ALFONSO. I don't care what corrupt dealings her spouse has with anybody! No favouritism here. The lady has no talent. I will not allow a tree to expire to satisfy her vanity. When I pronounce the word next, Jacqueline, that is exactly what I mean.

JACQUELINE (*looking inside a huge folder*). Alright, alright! 'Secret Gourmet Dishes from the Convent' by Sister Carolina.

DON ALFONSO. Now. In these monastic sauces, miss, there is no malice. No pollution, no aphrodisiacs, only natural herbs used. 200 copies recycled paper. Next?

The MAN *smiles, makes another gesture. Lights go down on him.*

JACQUELINE. 'Butcheries', a collection of poems by Lircay Santiago.

DON ALFONSO. Our salacious Lircay is in a bit of trouble. A thousand copies? What does he think we are – a paper factory?

JACQUELINE. You're forbidding him?

DON ALFONSO. Jacqueline: I detest the word forbid. We allocate scant resources, we set priorities, we make sure that the taxpayers are not subsidising smut. We never forbid.

JACQUELINE. Did you know that Lircay's wife is expecting their sixth child next month? Couldn't we allocate –

DON ALFONSO. Let nobody complain of my munificence.

JACQUELINE. Mugnificence?

DON ALFONSO. Cultivate your dictionary, my dear. Mu-ni-fi-cence. As for Lircay, tell him to put in an appearance – let's see, next Wednesday – so we can execute some editorial adjustments, a snip-snap here and there. But only a small grant.

JACQUELINE. What sort of adjustments?

DON ALFONSO. Take page 45, where it says – Oh if the moon could masturbate –

JACQUELINE (*taking notes*). – on page 45 where it says – does it really say that, Don Alfonso, on page 45?

DON ALFONSO. We could substitute: Oh if we might discern the uncertainty of sin in the waning moon.

JACQUELINE. Brilliant. You would have made one hell of a writer, I can tell you that.

DON ALFONSO *scratches the left side of his head with his right hand.*

DON ALFONSO. I am perfectly content with my present position, thank you. I had the writing fever when I was – I'll admit that, but now – what on earth would I be writing about now?

JACQUELINE. About you. And about . . . me. You. And me.

JACQUELINE *crosses to him, grabs his hand.* DON ALFONSO *quickly stands up, goes limping to the door of the office, opens it.*

DON ALFONSO. Miss, we have subscribed to a pact. I do not need to remind you that we are in a public place.

JACQUELINE (*going to door*). What is public can be transformed with the touch of a toe, darling (*She closes the door with her foot.*) into something extremely private. Today's Thursday.

JACQUELINE *takes one of his hands and puts it on her breast.*

And – what's this called, Alfonso?

DON ALFONSO (*withdrawing his hand*). That is called a – bosom.

JACQUELINE (*whispering*). Tit, my love, it's a darling tit. (*Louder.*) Such an expert with words, my Alfonsito, and you never manage to call things by their names.

She kisses him. DON ALFONSO *responds passionately. He disengages, gently sits her down in the chair, begins to limp to the door, stops when he hears* JACQUELINE's *next words.*

I bet you said 'tit' to – her. I bet you wrote poems to her, back when you wanted to be a writer, before you took this . . .

DON ALFONSO. What I used to converse with my wife is my business.

JACQUELINE. How about that other woman?

DON ALFONSO *scratches the left side of his head with his right hand.*

DON ALFONSO. What other woman?

JACQUELINE. A woman who came to ask for you this morning. She – well, seemed to know intimate details about you. The sort of things women know when –

DON ALFONSO. When what?

JACQUELINE. When she's . . . made love to a man. (*Pause.*) Passionately. With nothing between them but the skin she was born with. And even that's about to melt. Melt magnificently. Look it up in the dictionary. Magnificently.

DON ALFONSO. Who was it? Who was the woman?

JACQUELINE. It was . . . It was . . . Nobody.

DON ALFONSO. What do you mean, nobody?

JACQUELINE. A joke, you silly. I made her up. To see how you –

DON ALFONSO. I am not fond of your jokes.

JACQUELINE. Just wanted to see if you were hiding something from me, darling.

DON ALFONSO. Don't you darling me.

JACQUELINE. Just wanted to see if you trusted me.

There is a pause. DON ALFONSO *limps to the door, opens it.*

JACQUELINE. Your silence is eloquent.

DON ALFONSO. Silence is never eloquent, woman. Let me say no more. We have wasted enough time. To work. Our mission for today and every day: Making a tree happy . . .

JACQUELINE. Without making a writer sad. That's the mission for today – what about tonight's mission? Thursday night?

DON ALFONSO. It is not my impression, miss, that it is night-time. In fact there are exactly three hours and forty-six minutes before the sun sets today.

JACQUELINE. Why you even know the time the sun sets each day, Señor Morales. It's lucky for me that's not the only thing you know . . .

DON ALFONSO. It is lucky for you that I am – so fond of your idle prattle. Just remember: 'Power without . . . responsibility . . . '

JACQUELINE. Yeah, yeah, responsibility. 'Power without responsibility, the prerogative of the harlot through the ages.' I've heard it a thousand times. Stanley, Earl Baldwin, must have invented it while he was – you know what he must have been doing . . . Probably doing it to his secretary – and she was thinking, you know what she was thinking, while old Baldwin was humping away?

DON ALFONSO. How could I possibly know what she was thinking?

JACQUELINE *cuddles up to* DON ALFONSO, *provocative and ironic.*

JACQUELINE. 'Responsibility without power, the fate of the secretary through the ages.' You can quote me on it.

ENRIQUE MORALES *enters. He is dressed extravagantly, has a brash, expansive manner, almost hyper.*

ENRIQUE. Mot-mot, Pops. Jackie, my dear.

JACQUELINE *and* DON ALFONSO *separate, startled.*

I'm sure I'm not interrupting, as you did say you wanted to . . . . Urgent, you said. Five o'clock, you said.

DON ALFONSO. Yes, yes, of course. We've done our work for the day.

ENRIQUE. Are you sure? Saved enough trees? Made enough writers over-happy? What about this one?

ENRIQUE *goes to the desk, picks up a manuscript, opens it randomly towards the end.*

'Coming Together'. Intriguing title.

DON ALFONSO. Put that down.

ENRIQUE. Oh you know I don't read. Not me. Not us, Pops. We're into screens. Images? Mot, mot? Let's see. Maybe I've forgotten how to read. Not quite.

ENRIQUE *begins to read from the manuscript.*

(*Reading.*) '"Let me ask you something." The man's voice came from faraway, as if it were telegraphed instead of spoken. "Let me ask you something. If you had to choose between possessing a man's body and possessing his soul, what would you choose?"'

DON ALFONSO. I said to put that down.

ENRIQUE. Boring, boring! Just my luck. Possessing the soul? I was hoping for a steamy bedroom scene. I was hoping for naked bodies. Where've you got them stashed? Come on, confess.

DON ALFONSO. Stashed?

ENRIQUE. The hot stuff, Pops. You must have it all stashed away somewhere. We could divide the plunder. Look, I'll front for you.

DON ALFONSO. What are you talking about?

ENRIQUE. Purple eyes! I'm talking about pesos for purple eyes. How'd I look up there, strumming a guitar with my scalpel, Dr. Enrique Morales and his Purple Eyes Banda? Courtesy of my anthology – Howling virgins, depraved eunuchs, thrusting unicorns – My Anthology, Pops, remember? Forbidden Latino Readings – Come on, Pops, nobody would ever guess who was the real compiler of –

DON ALFONSO. You shouldn't even joke about these matters, Enrique. If the tree-police were to –

ENRIQUE. Who'd listen to me here? In the office of Mr. Loyalty? But you're right – point taken, mot-mot. Life is the only joke, but some things in it – like what can be done to our bodies – are serious as the smile of hell. Isn't that so, Jackie?

ENRIQUE *comes onto her.*

JACQUELINE. If you've finished with me, Don Alfonso . . . I've got some shopping to do for my mother. She hasn't been well lately.

DON ALFONSO *stands, limping slightly, and escorts her out.*

ENRIQUE. Hey, I can keep your Mama company, Jackie, I can do her shopping – and you can stay here with Pops. One happy family.

DON ALFONSO. Please accept my apologies for my son's behaviour, miss.

JACQUELINE. Don Alfonso, you're the last gentleman left in the world.

JACQUELINE exits angrily, closing the door. ENRIQUE *immediately changes his attitude, becomes reserved, serious, intent.*

DON ALFONSO. That was outrageous.

ENRIQUE. It was expedient.

DON ALFONSO. That is no way to treat a lady.

ENRIQUE. Don't try to give me lessons about how men should treat women.

DON ALFONSO. Oh, so that's what we're here for today?

ENRIQUE. You asked me to come. You tell me.

DON ALFONSO. No. You tell me. About this!

DON ALFONSO picks up the manuscript ENRIQUE *had been reading from.*

This preposterous futuristic novel. 'Coming Together'. Coming apart it should be – You insinuate yourself into this office with your sweet smiles, all charms, with the transparent subterfuge that one of your eternally unnamed friends wrote this trash, 'Could I have your opinion, Pops, could you authorise it for publication, *mot-mot*' – but I know who wrote it, I know who – and in fact, I don't know whether to be angrier because it's a bunch of irresponsible political claptrap and is going to land you and probably me in jail or if – what really hurts me, you want to know what really hurts me?

ENRIQUE. I didn't think anything could ever hurt you, Dad.

DON ALFONSO. What hurts me are the lies –

ENRIQUE. What lies?

A light comes up on the MAN. *He is standing behind the chair.* TANYA, *a young woman, is seated in it, bound and gagged. The* MAN *looks at* TANYA *and then at* DON ALFONSO *and* ENRIQUE *and then back again. A phone rings from the darkness.*

DON ALFONSO. The lies about your mother. How dare you imply that she – and it's you, not your fictitious friend, don't even try to deny it – that she died in a Readjustment Centre. You know she died at home. I was with her when she died. I held her hand.

ENRIQUE. I've been told differently.

DON ALFONSO. Yes – so you told me last night – to my face. But I never thought you'd go so far as to write your accusations down in a novel that you're asking me, me of all people, to authorise. God knows, maybe I've been hard on you, it hasn't been easy, Lord knows I've tried to be a mother and a father to you. But I am not a man who lies. Somebody is spreading stories about me, trying to destroy my reputation. And you're helping them. Look.

A phone rings again. Lights on ENRIQUE *begin to slowly fade.* DON ALFONSO *leafs through the novel, shows it to his son.*

ENRIQUE (*almost a shadow*). I have proof, Dad. How could you do it? Why did you send her there to die? What did you fear?

The phone is still ringing. ENRIQUE *begins to exit.*

DON ALFONSO (*shouting*). Answer that Goddamned phone!

Lights disappear on MAN *and* TANYA. *Bright, cheerful Lights rise on the office and the anteroom adjoined to it.* ENRIQUE *disappears into the darkness.* IRENE, *played by the same actress who plays* JACQUELINE, *is working. She answers the phone. We are in* DANIEL LUCAS's *office in the Moral Resources Company in the far future. All of a sudden, under a different light, everything seems more futuristic, the furniture and the desk high-tech. Through the window where we saw verdant luxury, there now pulse electronic, psychedelic images. The umbrella becomes a decoration.* DON ALFONSO *is transformed into* DANIEL LUCAS, *seated at his desk, rigid. He scratches the right side of his head with his left hand.*

DANIEL LUCAS (*reading from the manuscript*). '"What did you fear?" And Don Alfonso Morales answered his son with his favourite word of the last twenty years: "Nothing." ' Nothing. Nothing, huh?

IRENE *presses a button. An intercom buzzes.* DANIEL LUCAS *ignores it, keeps reading.*

'All his Latino life, Don Alfonso Morales had proclaimed that dreams are meaningless. Someday the species would overcome this annoying habit of the mind as it had successfully defeated the need to walk on all fours. And yet he had dreamt last night this very encounter with his son.'

Another buzz. DANIEL *answers the intercom.*

Is that you, Irene?

IRENE. Who did you expect, Mr. Lucas? Christopher Columbus?

DANIEL LUCAS. Your jokes get funnier every day, Irene. What is it?

IRENE. Your son Nick is on the way. Just as you asked, Mr. Lucas. And Bergante just called. He wanted to know if you'd already read the manuscript by David Malko he –

DANIEL LUCAS. He must have psychic powers. I'm reading it now.

IRENE. So? What d'you think?

DANIEL LUCAS. It's a . . . – If that damn Bergante would cease interrupting me, I would by now have determined if we can green-light this project. Tell him that.

IRENE. Right. I'll tell him that.

DANIEL LUCAS. No – wait! About the author, this Malko person – ask Bergante . . . . his name.

IRENE. We know his name. David Malko.

DANIEL LUCAS. Well, I thought this Malko – he might be – you know, a pseudonym.

IRENE. I'll ask Bergante. Anything else?

DANIEL LUCAS. Could you – join me for a few minutes, there's something . . . there's something . . .

IRENE. Disturbing you?

DANIEL LUCAS. Yes.

IRENE *enters, closing the door.*

The door, the door. Miss, we have subscribed to a pact. I do not need – I do not need –

IRENE. You do not need . . . ?

DANIEL LUCAS (*recomposing himself*). In fact, it's good you closed the door. For once, you have been foresightful. Because I – it's this damned manuscript that Bergante sent me to see if we could authorise an option, it's –

IRENE. 'Turns' by David Malko?

DANIEL LUCAS. I haven't finished it yet but –

IRENE. Well, Bergante says it doesn't have an ending yet. That's why he sent it to you, to see if you could suggest – some rewrites that would –

DANIEL LUCAS. I have no suggestions. The author is obviously one of those spoiled young people who take pure bodies, pure thoughts, a pure planet for granted without ever pondering the sacrifices we made to get here. Take notes.

IRENE. Mr. Lucas . . .

DANIEL LUCAS. I'll use these thoughts for the speech I'm giving at the BookSellers Association when they honour my Twenty Years of Moral Service to Art. I'll tell them about these youngsters who hardly know how to write any more and don't have memories of how things were before – when the great plague was raging, violence and sex on every screen – so the minor sacrifices and restrictions that seem natural to older people look unnecessary to them. Are you taking notes?

IRENE. Mr. Lucas. Are you sure we're talking about the same book? Bergante says it happens a long time ago, in a small impoverished Spanish-American country, he said – and there's an ecofascist dictatorship, a terrible place according to – And we've got democracy, so how can – ?

DANIEL LUCAS. Would you cease your cackling, woman? This Malko fellow, he's a clever one – he's set it far away, long ago, riding the ecological fad to snipe at us. Look – he's breaking every guideline in sight. Twenty-second kisses on screen. A hand on a – bosom. A man and a woman in the same bed together. Let me say no more.

IRENE. Before, during or after?

DANIEL LUCAS. After. But that's not what – what –

IRENE. Disturbs you? We can fix the kisses. Cut them to the regulatory two seconds.

DANIEL LUCAS. Stop defending the bastard. Look – in this script there's a certain Don Alfonso Morales, he's a – censor – in some sort of – it's some sort of Office or Library or Ministry back then that controls the flow of books – an absurd premise, though I have read that in certain poor countries during the twentieth century paper was rationed supposedly to save the forests – but of course it was merely a sham for them to export all the trees while the thought police controlled the – Listen, Irene, this pompous idiot of a censor – his son Enrique – Enrique's a medical student who's secretly written a book that irresponsibly accuses the – but what matters is that this man's wife – the Morales man, not his son, – it's the man's wife who really – and if the son's suspicions – but of course the son's in danger –

IRENE. You've got to excuse me, Mr. Lucas, but you're really – why, you're rambling!

DANIEL LUCAS. Listen to this. 'Don Alfonso Morales scratched his left ear. And he scratched it, as usual, with his right hand.' Well . . . ?

IRENE. Well, what?

DANIEL LUCAS. Doesn't this palely – remind you of somebody?

DANIEL LUCAS *scratches his right ear with his left hand.*

IRENE (*laughing*). You think that . . .

DANIEL LUCAS. Yes.

IRENE. You really think that somebody has . . . That this Malko who you don't even know . . .

DANIEL LUCAS. Yes.

IRENE. You could be wrong. After all, you scratch your right ear with your left hand, Daniel, so –

DANIEL LUCAS. No. The man – there are other parallels that –

IRENE. Well, congratulations, then. How does it feel, to be a hero in –

DANIEL LUCAS. The man's not a hero. He's a – I don't want that Alfonso Morales out there for anybody to see, my co-facilitators would crucify me – Why, the man's – detestable. He's a – a censor for a brutal tyranny. And he's – Latin-American. And – he limps! The bastard is a cripple. In body. And in mind. An unfeeling son of a bitch.

IRENE. Then he's got nothing to do with you – Your legs are magnificently sturdy – and you should –

DANIEL LUCAS. Magnificently. Right. Except that in other things –

IRENE. – So why should you . . . I mean, Nick's not in trouble, is he?

DANIEL LUCAS. Certainly not.

IRENE. So you're just imagining things. And maybe you should give the project a green light, so nobody can say you're prejudiced against something that seems so close to home, so to speak. Maybe if we suggest some rewrites and allow this Malko to resubmit. Because sponsors have been demanding more dramas with Latino themes – and if we can get a crippled actor to do the role of this Morales guy, then –

DANIEL LUCAS. No.

IRENE. How about a reading with Latino actors to see if – ?

DANIEL LUCAS. No.

IRENE. Not even conditionally denied production, so he – ?

DANIEL LUCAS. No, no, no. Nothing whatsoever.

Abruptly the DIRECTOR *enters out of nowhere.*

DIRECTOR. Is this music to my ears? Or disharmony? A stream of negatives. Interdictions. Denials. No, no, no. Nothing whatsoever. It's good to keep the standards and the practices high – but let's hope we're not keeping juicy cultural material from the viewers, Luke.

DANIEL LUCAS. We're here to serve the viewers, sir.

DIRECTOR. And the sponsors. Thirsting for the newest. So I should not interrupt –

DANIEL LUCAS. The Director of Moral Resources is always welcome in this office.

DIRECTOR. I'd better be. Because I've been protecting you, Luke. You're one lucky bastard. D' you know that? D' you know what your co-facilitators call you? (*Pause.*) What do they call you? (*Pause.*)

IRENE (*blurting it out*). The Pope.

DIRECTOR (*looks her over*). 'Cause he's infallible, right? 'Cause you're infallible, Danny Lucas. How long have we . . . ?

DANIEL LUCAS. Twenty years, sir.

DIRECTOR. Twenty years and you haven't made one mistake. That's a great nickname. (*Pause.*) Give me a hint, Luke, a hint, a clue, an inkling, tell me. You've authorised more scripts than anyone else in this building, anonymously bestowed more production slips, rewritten endings, doctored scenes, more than – Has one of the shows you originated ever been denounced as pornographic? Have the Supreme Justices of Preservation ever accused you of wasting our moral and bodily resources?

We hear a series of melodious chimes in the air. The DIRECTOR *immediately stops talking and turns to* DANIEL LUCAS, *gives him a hug, then hugs* IRENE, *then* IRENE *hugs* DANIEL LUCAS, *then all three stand there smiling happily. The chimes continue for a few more beats, then die out. The three return to their former positions.*

Don't you just love the Smiley Minute? Makes you feel so – upbeat, so – But where was I?

IRENE . . . . wasting our moral and bodily resources . . .

DIRECTOR. Right, correct, absolutely. That's it. Has this Production Company ever been sued by a husband because one of our programs induced his wife to adultery? And the ratings – have we ever lost one ratings sweep since you joined us? The Pope? Ha! That's what they used to call me. At about the time

I discovered you. The Pope? Old Eagle Eyes, that's what they
call you. How d' you do it, Luke? How in hell do you – ?
What's the secret?

DANIEL LUCAS. There is no secret, Director. It's merely a
matter of – culture, taste I suppose we could call it.

DIRECTOR. Show me.

DANIEL LUCAS. Show you what, sir?

DIRECTOR. How you do it. Take anything – this manuscript, for
instance – 'Turns' – by David Malko . . . ?

DANIEL LUCAS. I think this one's not ready, not quite –

DIRECTOR. Better yet. Maybe we can give the writer some
pointers.

DANIEL LUCAS. There are more stimulating texts than –

DIRECTOR (*ignoring him*). Take this dialogue. (*To* IRENE.)
Come here, my dear, and help me out. You'll do the woman
and I'll do the man – unless, of course, you'd like to reverse
positions?

IRENE. I'll do the woman.

DIRECTOR. By all means. Let me see now. Why, there's a
Director in this novel. Hey, maybe I could do a cameo – play
myself, you know.

DANIEL LUCAS. I don't think you would care to play that role,
sir. The man's a bit of – a villain.

DIRECTOR. Better to play the villain in a movie than to be a
villain in reality. Now, let's see: *The Director watched the face
of a woman emerge from the shadows, as if from the darkness
of the dead.* Well, that's not a bad way of beginning a scene.
Suspense, huh, tension, apprehension. Then this man, he says:
'You haven't aged,' that's what the Director – 'Why, look at
you, you're still a girl. What have you been doing with yourself, to your little self, to stop time?' Hmmm. Not quite original,
to greet someone that way, but – you can't always be snappy,
I guess.

DANIEL LUCAS. It is meant as a metaphor, sir, I believe.
Ironically.

DIRECTOR. Why's that?

DANIEL LUCAS. The woman in question – she was thought to be
dead.

DIRECTOR. Dead?

DANIEL LUCAS. In a manner of speaking, sir. Interned for life in a – one of these mental institutions.

DIRECTOR. Like one of our Readjustment Centres?

DANIEL LUCAS. Yes, sir. So to greet her in that way . . .

DIRECTOR. Aha! A metaphor! I see. This is getting interesting. Now it's your turn, Irene. Here. 'I've been waiting for my boy to grow up. So he can learn the truth.'

IRENE (*reading*). 'I've been waiting for my boy to grow up. So he can learn the truth.'

DIRECTOR (*reading*). 'He'll never believe you. He adores his father.'

DANIEL LUCAS *watches the scene in great agitation.*

IRENE (*reading*). 'That's why I'm going to make his father tell him the truth.'

DIRECTOR (*reading*). 'You're crazy.'

IRENE (*reading*). 'Yes, I know. That's what the limping bastard said to me. And that Judge – when he stopped me from seeing my boy, he said the same thing: "Anybody who isn't happy in Paradise must be crazy." And dangerous. And he was right. I am dangerous. So you'd better watch out.'

DIRECTOR. Watch out. Watch out, huh? That's good advice for all of us. So – what do you think? Luke?

DANIEL LUCAS (*dazed*). What?

DIRECTOR. Not badly written. And life-like, huh? And Latinos. We could fulfil our quota. What d'you think? Should we give this Malko a chance?

DANIEL LUCAS *turns, as if in a trance.*

IRENE. I believe Mr. Lucas told you that he hasn't formed an opinion yet, sir.

DIRECTOR (*looks her over again*). Well, we have to be extra careful. We're being watched. We've got to authorise more, so our enemies can't accuse us of not being liberal enough. And we've got to authorise less, so they can't accuse us of not being conservative enough. We're at a critical moment. Happy but critical. Because there's only one problem with Paradise – one problem: people get bored. (*Pause.*) Some sponsors are worried because we're too lusty, risqué, racy, you know, and other sponsors are worried because we're too traditional, not enough new stuff. But they're all united in one common cause, right, Irene?

IRENE (*as if reciting a litany*). To never forget how the plague started, to heed that warning and take our punishment, because next time there may not be a next time.

DIRECTOR (*joining in at the end*). There may not be a next time. Right! So we have to show where we stand. If you get my meaning?

DANIEL LUCAS. So this script. You wish me to . . . ?

DIRECTOR. Your son.

DANIEL LUCAS. What about – my – ?

DIRECTOR. Not married yet, I take it, since the last time I inquired?

DANIEL LUCAS. No, sir, you may remember he obtained a deferral due to his – He's graduating from Medicine this –

DIRECTOR. Yes – if he's studying so hard that would explain why his happy signature isn't in yet. You know, the –

IRENE. Mr. Lucas is perfectly aware of the marriage signature, sir, the one that had to be ready –

The DIRECTOR *steers* IRENE *towards the door, speaks as she is ushered out of the room.*

IRENE. Alright, alright. I have to go and feed my cat anyway. Today's . . . Thursday.

She exits and remains on the other side of the anteroom door, trying to listen to the conversation.

DANIEL LUCAS. By noon tomorrow, of course. I've had Irene ask my son to come and see me, so his signature . . .

DIRECTOR. Leave his patients? That's what I call devotion.

DANIEL LUCAS. The marriage signature is not to be taken lightly –

DIRECTOR. Our employees agree. They've enrolled all eligible sons and daughters – eager to provide us with ample, plentiful families. No free-love conspiracy for them, no sabotaging the repopulation of our depleted species, no, sir, they're not insulting the bodies of God by filling themselves with pills and devices and unhappy contraceptives. No abortions for them. Brownie points, Luke, they're accumulating brownie points. But your son –

DANIEL LUCAS. Nicholas.

DIRECTOR. That's the one! – his signature is particularly . . . Because – Can you keep a secret? Can you? Well, I'm moving up, Luke. Up, up, up.

DANIEL LUCAS. How far up, sir?

DIRECTOR (*whispering*). SuperDirector. SuperPope. So –

DANIEL LUCAS. So . . . ?

DIRECTOR. So you're in the running to take over my present post. Top of the list. Unless –

DANIEL LUCAS. Unless . . . ?

DIRECTOR. Well, we can expect a lot of extra scrutiny in the days ahead, Luke. Ways in which your loyalty gets tested, you know, people going over your past with a comb to make sure that . . . But you don't have anything to worry about, do you?

DANIEL LUCAS. So those people, sir, they will be asking questions about . . . about my wife, sir?

DIRECTOR. What wife?

DANIEL LUCAS. My – former wife. Tanya.

DIRECTOR. What's there to ask about her?

DANIEL LUCAS. Well, that depends, sir – I mean, perhaps you've spoken – recently, I mean – to somebody about her . . .

DIRECTOR. Fuck them, Danny. Fuck them if they're spreading vile stories. Look, when I found you – there you were, trying to get an irrelevant book published, squandering your skills, freezing on the edge of the edge, farming your young Nick out to relatives – and mad, wild, Tanya, did she care? Did she know where your real talents lay, that you could be a father to millions of defenceless people who needed a guardian to their dreams? But I knew.

DIRECTOR *sits* DANIEL *down in his chair.*

DIRECTOR. And I also knew there was one slight problem to overcome if you were to give me your unerring eyes, your then young eagle eyes, one problem to overcome if you were to join us in our crusade. One problem.

DANIEL LUCAS. I don't like to talk about this.

DIRECTOR. Right! So why are we talking about this? About her? Why aren't we talking about – Paradise: lots of trees, lots of babies, lots of salvation, no boredom. If I were you, Luke, I would concentrate on important things: such as making sure this story of ours has a happy ending.

The DIRECTOR *exits.* DANIEL LUCAS *scratches the right side of his head with his left hand and then looks at it as if he did not recognise it. He opens the manuscript. Behind him, the* MAN *and* TANYA *appear.* TANYA *is still in the chair. The* MAN *takes the gag off her.*

DANIEL LUCAS (*reading*). 'There is only one way out. Tell him. Tell him what happened.'

TANYA. There is only one way out. Tell him. Tell him what happened to me.

DANIEL *abruptly slams the text closed. The* MAN *disappears from view, along with* TANYA. TANYA's *voice comes out of the darkness.*

TANYA's VOICE. It's the only way.

DANIEL *hesitantly, reluctantly, opens the text again, peeks at it.* NICK *enters the anteroom. He is played by the same actor who played* ENRIQUE, *but conservatively dressed. He enters* DANIEL's *office.* DANIEL *looks up, startled.* NICK *goes over to give his father a hug.* DANIEL *nervously puts the manuscript away.*

NICK. Well, aren't we secretive today?

DANIEL LUCAS. Yes. Some of us are.

NICK. So – what's up? I've left three dying patients to . . .

DANIEL LUCAS. David Malko. Your friend David Malko. Tell me about him.

NICK. Never heard of.

DANIEL LUCAS (*more and more agitated*). You must know him, have talked to him at some point. Think. A writer called Malko! You told him something about my – my habits, my – wife.

NICK. Your wife?

DANIEL LUCAS. My life. You described me. Think!

NICK. My Lord, who is this Malko person who's got you so – ?

DANIEL LUCAS. Somebody's been talking about me to him – somebody's been telling him that I – What have you told your friends about me?

NICK. Nothing. Your favourite word, Dad. Nothing.

DANIEL LUCAS. Nothing, nothing. You never whispered a word about me?

NICK. The most I've ever told anybody is that you're one serious guy – serious as the smile of hell, in fact.

DANIEL LUCAS. Serious as the smile of hell? Wait. You – Malko. You got that stupid phrase from him.

NICK. It's a song, Dad. Everybody sings it. What's there to fear? What's there to fear? Nothing is as serious as the smile of hell. It is sort of stupid, but . . .

DANIEL LUCAS. You're not telling me the – In here, in this novel, there's a young man who has spent his whole life making believe he – but he's involved in . . .

NICK. Involved in what?

DANIEL LUCAS . . . . involved in something, like you – you know, with your friends. No matter what it is – you can trust me, it hasn't been easy, I've tried to be a father –

NICK. Yes, Dad – and a mother, I know. But what is it that I'm supposed to have –

DANIEL LUCAS. Don't say it. Not another word. Not in here. They're watching us.

NICK. Here? In the office of Mr. Loyalty? Who's –

DANIEL. The tree police.

NICK. What tree police? Hey what's –

The intercom buzzes.

DANIEL LUCAS (*answering*). Oh, yes, Director . . . . He's here right now. I'll get it as soon as I hang up, sir. Yes. Tomorrow at noon.

DANIEL LUCAS *hangs up, turns to* NICK.

Well, here's your chance. He wants the marriage signature. Before noon tomorrow. You sign and that proves that all my suspicions are wrong.

NICK. What suspicions? Just because I'm not sure about this marriage thing – Yesterday we had agreed that we could defer –

DANIEL LUCAS. We can't wait. No more deferments. I'm – being tested. You have to sign. Or they'll –

NICK. They'll what? Listen, Dad, if that computer makes a –

DANIEL LUCAS. The computer never makes a mistake. It unfailingly matches the right young man with the right young woman. Right genes, right attitudes, right breeding yields the right children. Look at you. Look at your mother and me, look at how well that –

NICK. How can you be sure?

DANIEL LUCAS. What do you mean?

NICK. Was it really that successful, your marriage?

DANIEL LUCAS. How can you ask me that? You know that she died holding my hand, that we – Who's been telling you . . . ?

NICK. C'mon, Dad. Nobody's been – I just asked you because,

well, she did die young, before you had a chance to find out if
it was going to – Nobody's told me a thing.

DANIEL. I don't deserve this runaround. Somebody's out to get
me, Nick, and if they're spreading rumours – Nick! Please,
I need to know.

NICK hands a photo to DANIEL LUCAS, who examines it.

NICK. Mom's photo. I think it's her photo. It arrived this morning,
Dad. In the mail. I decided I wouldn't even bring it to your –
but if there's a campaign to – Look at what's written on the
other side.

DANIEL LUCAS (*turns it over, reads*). 'Once upon a time there
was a man who was afraid.' Afraid? Afraid of what? What is
this? Some sort of sick joke? Who wrote this?

NICK (*calmly*). You tell me. Is there something you're afraid of?

DANIEL LUCAS (*agitated*). Nothing, nothing.

NICK. Then there's no reason to be this upset, right? Unless –
unless . . . There is something you – something to do with
Mom. Why else would somebody go to all the trouble of
finding her photo and then sending it and then – Dad? Is there
something you're afraid of?

Lights begin to fade on NICK.

DANIEL LUCAS (*barely in control*). I told you. Nothing. You
heard me. I said nothing. Nothing. Nothing. Nothing. My God –
I've got to get out of here.

NICK (*almost a shadow*). Is there something you haven't – Did
something – did something happen to my mother?

DANIEL. I've got to get out of this. I – your mother, your mother.
I've got to get out.

NICK disappears.

NICK's VOICE. Dad? What happened to my mother?

*On the other side of the stage, the MAN emerges from the
darkness. He makes a gesture. And TANYA appears, seated,
but not tied or gagged. When the MAN speaks, it is casually.*

MAN. I've been thinking about pain. There is good pain and there
is bad pain. Good pain is at the origin of all knowledge, it's –
good for you. Knowing where we begin and others end. There
are good borders and then there are bad borders. Borders that
preserve who we are and borders that let in the germs of who
we are not. So when boundaries are violated, when rules are
broken, just remember there's somebody like me who's there.
At the edge. You fuck with the edge. You fuck with me.

Lights go down on the office. A spot on DANIEL, *who doesn't move. He is paralysed by fear. He clutches the umbrella in his hand as if it were a weapon.*

TANYA's VOICE (*from the darkness*). There is only one way out.

The office disappears. The MAN *gently invites* TANYA *out of her chair, he steps back into the darkness, she slowly comes forward towards* DANIEL *in his spot of light. She puts her hands over his eyes playfully.*

TANYA. Alfonso. Alfonso. I know a way out.

DANIEL LUCAS. Tanya?

DANIEL LUCAS *turns. They kiss. She disengages, walks away from him.* DANIEL LUCAS *begins to limp behind her, holding the umbrella, lights swirl around him murkily. He becomes* DON ALFONSO.

TANYA. There's only one way out. Tell him, Alfonso. Tell him what happened to me.

DON ALFONSO. No.

TANYA. Yes. It's the only way.

Tell him, yes, how the woman you loved was in the way. Tell him how your marriage started to break down when you accepted this job, yes, that the woman you loved couldn't stand to see you suppress the better part of yourself. And then tell him how they asked for proof of your loyalty. What you did to her to prove your loyalty.

DON ALFONSO. That's not how it was.

TANYA. If you once loved . . . .

DON ALFONSO. Yes. A long time ago – I loved someone. But there's nothing left. I can't even remember what it felt like.

TANYA. Do you remember that poem? You read it to me the first time we made love. I was so unsure of what was in the pit of your mind and you answered: 'Love consists of this / A dialogue of solitudes.' Don't be afraid. For once in your life, don't be afraid.

DON ALFONSO. Why are you saying that to me again? Why did you always say that to me?

TANYA. I said it so you wouldn't betray me.

DON ALFONSO (*to himself, whispering*). It's not true. She was the one. She was the one who betrayed me – by hating what I – by not even trying to cooperate. And why the hell was she there anyway? That day. That day I came home and Tanya was there. I don't know how she got in. I didn't even ask her. Crazy: she was combing her hair. (*To* TANYA, *who has started to comb her long hair.*) What are you doing here?

TANYA. I'm making myself pretty to see my little boy.

DON ALFONSO. He'll be back from school any time now. Get out before –

TANYA. They know who I am. They can see under my face. Here – touch the plague under my face. Touch me here, under my face and feel the –

DON ALFONSO. You're crazy.

TANYA. Anybody who isn't happy in Paradise must be crazy, right? That's what that Judge said when he stopped me from seeing my boy. But that wasn't enough for you, was it?

DON ALFONSO. You need help. Professional help.

TANYA. Well, they came for me this morning. Your friend the Director He was with them. He had my signature. Confessing. Accepting my guilt. Accepting that I would spend the rest of my life in a loony –

DON ALFONSO. Don't call it that.

TANYA. Only it wasn't my signature. Guess who signed for me?

DON ALFONSO. I did it to save you. They would have dragged it out of you. They would have hurt you.

TANYA. So that's what you said to yourself when you signed for me. In the name of others, in the name of Paradise – isn't that what they always say? Over and over again in history, isn't that the excuse? For the good of others?

The MAN *appears out of the darkness with the chair, sets it down, steps back, watches the scene.* TANYA *and* DANIEL *do not see him.*

DON ALFONSO. Yes, Tanya – it was for your good. They would have come for you anyway and I –

TANYA. They don't know where I am now.

DON ALFONSO. Then you'd better leave before they find out.

TANYA. Not until I've said good-bye to my boy. Not until I've told him the truth.

DON ALFONSO. You never knew when to stop. You asked for it.

DON ALFONSO *turns his back on* TANYA, *takes a cellular phone out of his pocket, begins to speak. She circles him, trying to catch his eye while he continues to turn his back.*

DON ALFONSO. Get me the Director.

TANYA. I wouldn't call him if I were you.

DON ALFONSO. Ah, Director. Not too well, I'm afraid. In fact, I'm having a spot of trouble – the bitch is right here, in fact.

TANYA. You're not going to stop me.

DON ALFONSO. I'll keep her here, Director. Just hurry.

TANYA. No. No. I won't let you shut me up – I won't, I won't –

DON ALFONSO (*turns to her*). Shut up, you dirty cunt.

He hangs up and takes off his tie. A violent struggle. He forces her into the chair and then starts to gag her with the tie.

TANYA (*gasping for breath*). You crippled son of a bitch! I'll be back for my boy.

DON ALFONSO (*overlapping*). Shut up, shut up, shut up.

TANYA. I'll tell him what –

DON ALFONSO *finishes gagging her.*

DON ALFONSO. Now tell him the truth, you bitch.

Lights begin to go down on TANYA *in her chair. Suddenly, the* DIRECTOR *surges forward. He stands next to* TANYA, *looks at* DON ALFONSO *for a few beats, then drags her away into the darkness.* DON ALFONSO *watches, shocked. He staggers backward, into the space of the darkened office. As the lights change, he becomes* DANIEL LUCAS *again.*

NICK's VOICE (*from the darkness*). I asked you a question.

The lights return to normal.

DANIEL LUCAS. What question?

NICK. What happened to my mother?

DANIEL LUCAS. Nothing. Nothing. What I always told you. She died in our house. I was holding her hand when she –

NICK. Yes, yes, I've heard it all before – how you tried to be a father and a mother to me. Only not this time. This time I know you're hiding something.

DANIEL. You mustn't believe the stories people are – circulating. I have enemies. They don't want me to be promoted, they –

NICK. Maybe they know something I should know.

DANIEL. Excuse me. I have work to do. I can be monitored at any moment to see if my work is satisfactory.

DANIEL *picks up the manuscript, begins to sharpen a pencil: empty gestures to avoid looking at* NICK.

NICK. Dad? Dad? Whoever sent that photo knows. He'll tell me. He'll tell me what happened to my mother.

NICK *exits. Lights begin to go down leaving a strong beam on* DANIEL LUCAS.

DANIEL LUCAS. Lies, Nick. All lies.

DANIEL LUCAS's VOICE. So you thought you knew him, Alfonso? You brought him up, but did you know him, that motherless mystery of a young man?

DANIEL LUCAS *slowly begins to undress, crossing the stage to a bed that has appeared.*

DANIEL LUCAS's VOICE. He's farther from you than the remotest star, farther from you than your own image reflected in the only eyes that want to reflect your tired features, Jacqueline's loyal eyes. And Don Alfonso Morales remembered without enthusiasm . . .

IRENE *appears at the edge of the bed, in a nightgown. She gets into the bed. She takes off her nightgown.* DANIEL LUCAS *stands next to the bed. He gets into it. Total darkness. As we hear* IRENE's VOICE *picking up the narrative, we can also hear the sounds of frustrated love-making,* DANIEL *saying: I can't, I can't,* IRENE *urging him on,* DANIEL *cursing,* IRENE *trying to calm him down.*

IRENE's VOICE. And Don Alfonso remembered without enthusiasm that he was scheduled to meet Jacqueline again – another monotonous Thursday night encounter he would honour only because our fearful friend had no other unfortunate body in this desolate universe to welcome him. And he realised that he didn't trust her, that he could not tell her his most secret thoughts. That he did not love her.

DANIEL LUCAS's VOICE (*from the darkness*). I'm sorry. God, I'm sorry.

IRENE's VOICE (*from the darkness*). What's there to be sorry about?

DANIEL LUCAS's VOICE (*from the darkness*). Well – the thing didn't – you know – well – work.

DANIEL LUCAS *flicks the lamp on.*

IRENE. Does it matter that much? Men are always so worried about –

DANIEL LUCAS. Don't try to disguise that I was not quite up to standards.

IRENE. You were – well, strange, if you're so hot to know. As if I were making love with – well, trying to make love – with someone I had just met.

DANIEL LUCAS. So you also found me strange?

IRENE. Somebody else found you strange?

DANIEL LUCAS. Nicholas.

IRENE. What sort of – performance did he complain about?

DANIEL LUCAS. That's not funny. My performance with you was not what might be – expected, simply because of that infernal novel.

IRENE. Mr. Malko's?

DANIEL LUCAS. That's the culprit.

IRENE. It's his real name. Not a pseudonym. And I got you the address.

She hands a piece of paper to DANIEL LUCAS.

Here it is. Hasn't got a phone. Lives out in the slums. No job. Had to ship his kid to his wife's parents because they couldn't afford to – They barely get by on what his wife –

DANIEL LUCAS. So our friend Malko's not doing too well.

DANIEL LUCAS *starts to dress.*

IRENE. You seem to enjoy the idea that he's in trouble.

DANIEL LUCAS. Yes, I do. I hope he's in bushels of trouble. What right does the rascal have to inject me into his libellous book? Or to steal my thoughts, my most secret thoughts.

IRENE. Well. (*Pause.*) Maybe there's a little something in Malko's novel you're keeping from me? Let's forget the monotonous Thursday encounters and the unfortunate body. Here. Don Alfonso is – thinking – ha!- to himself. (IRENE *reads from a piece of paper.*) 'Got to go and see Jacqueline now. She's possessive and obtuse – but at least she's got splendid breasts. If I cared for her . . . ' Now, what's this to do with us? The breasts, I'll accept that part of it, I rather like that part, but possessive and obtuse . . . and then it says he doesn't love her . . .

DANIEL LUCAS. Care for her.

IRENE. Always correcting, always correcting. Care for her, love her. You underlined that part.

DANIEL LUCAS. I merely underlined it because it was one of the few places that did not fit me, fit our little –

IRENE. So where she says, You don't trust me. That has nothing
to do with us? I read that too, Daniel – and it – Maybe this
story's telling me that you're – You don't trust me, do you?

*Thunder. Outside the room, under a murky ghostly light, two
shadows begin to emerge, one seated in a chair, the other
behind the chair. We cannot see who they are.*

As she says: Your silence is eloquent.

DANIEL LUCAS. Silence is never eloquent, woman – Oh my
God – You're the one. I know, I know: now you're going to tell
me that the bitch came today to –

IRENE. What bitch came today?

DANIEL LUCAS. You're the one. You're the one who –

IRENE. I'm the one who what? What am I doing except hitching
my ass to a man who won't marry me?

DANIEL LUCAS. You're the one who's been telling them.
About Tanya.

IRENE. About Tanya?

DANIEL LUCAS. About me, about me.

IRENE (*derisively*). Sorry to contradict you, honey, but that theory
won't hold water, not a drop of it. Why would I want to screw
up our relationship more. It's already in enough trouble. If
you're looking for someone you'd never suspect –

*Thunder. Rain starts. DANIEL turns to the window. Outside,
one of the shadows turns into NICK, seated in the same chair
TANYA occupied before, gagged and tied like she was, under
a beam of white light. Behind him, the MAN.*

IRENE. . . . How about Nick?

DANIEL LUCAS *is upset, peering at the shadows.*

IRENE. I mean, what if Nick is – well, involved in something?
Following orders – you know, from the free-love conspiracy or
some other nutty organisation?

MAN (*to* NICK). So you want to know what happened to your
mother, huh? Well, I never had a mother. So I guess I'm in a
position to tell you what happened to yours. Wouldn't you say?
If you could say? Or maybe, if you could say something, you'd
like to tell me something else. Before you find out what
happened to your mother.

DANIEL LUCAS. No. No. Leave him alone. Don't –

MAN (*to* NICK). Just remember: I'm your friend. Your only friend.

IRENE. What's the matter, Daniel?

DANIEL LUCAS (*moving towards the door*). I'll save him.
I won't let . . .

*Lights dim slightly on IRENE as she starts dressing and
DANIEL LUCAS rushes out. NICK and the MAN suddenly
disappear, leaving the rain and the silence. A long pause. The
rain stops. Suddenly, the DIRECTOR appears. DANIEL
LUCAS crosses to him.*

DANIEL LUCAS. Director, Director!

DIRECTOR. I'm not the damn director of anything.

DANIEL LUCAS. In that case, you must – excuse me, sir. I must
be – I haven't been – well lately –

DIRECTOR. These things happen. Mistaken identities, I mean.
I've been confused before with somebody else.

DANIEL LUCAS. Alright, sir, I get it – it's a test, I understand.

DIRECTOR. I hate tests. Ever since school. When I had to get my
father's signature on every lousy test. He beat the shit out of
me. All because of a signature.

DANIEL LUCAS. The signature. Of course. Noon. Tomorrow.
My Nick's a good boy, sir, a bit stubborn, you know, young
people –

DIRECTOR. I don't know any young people. But it sounds to me
as if this little Nick of yours is in trouble. As if he's up to no
good.

DANIEL LUCAS. I'm afraid I don't understand.

DIRECTOR. You're afraid. Good for you. Fear is the root of all
wisdom.

*The DIRECTOR exits. DANIEL LUCAS makes an attempt to
follow – then stops. IRENE, having dressed, joins him in the
street.*

DANIEL LUCAS (*to IRENE, wildly*). The Director – the Director
– He was just here, he – He's after my boy, he's –

IRENE. You must be dreaming. The Director has a chauffeur. And
why would he be on the streets looking for Nick?

DANIEL LUCAS. He said he wasn't the Director, but –

IRENE. You see.

DANIEL LUCAS. It's that damn book. It's driving me crazy. I'm
– seeing things.

IRENE. Trap the bastard!

DANIEL LUCAS. The Director?

IRENE. Malko. David Malko. Listen, honey, if somebody were fucking with my identity, I'd tear their eyes out. Let's track him down, this Malko bastard, find out who he's working for, who's feeding him his information. Your co-facilitators, or Nick, or – who knows –

DANIEL LUCAS. Track him down?

The sound of a typewriter. Lights rise on the Malko house, showing it to be sombre and poor. The silhouette of a woman appears, typing. We cannot distinguish her face yet.

DANIEL LUCAS. Irene, I'm going to do it. They want to drive me mad? Well, I'll do something mad, something they'll – I'll find out if Nick is part of this – this – (*Speaking as he walks towards the Malko house.*) Cover for me at the office. I'll be back as soon as I find out who's been spying on me, writing me down, who it is, and why. As soon as I –

IRENE. As soon as you – what, my love?

DANIEL LUCAS *has reached the Malko door.*

DANIEL LUCAS. As soon I find out how this damn story ends.

DANIEL LUCAS *knocks on the door. The lights go up on SONIA, typing. She is played by the same actress who plays TANYA, except her hair is tucked away with a scarf. She wears heavy winter clothes, as if it were very cold and there were no heating in the room. Another knock. Total darkness.*

End of Act One.

ACT TWO

In the darkness, the sound of typing. Then, knocking. Lights rise on
DANIEL LUCAS *in front of* MALKO's *house. Another knock.*
The sound of typing stops. Another knock. We can vaguely see the
figure of a man, also wrapped in heavy clothes, next to SONIA.
He is DAVID MALKO, *but we cannot yet distinguish his face.*

DAVID (*whispering, shivering*). Don't open.

SONIA (*whispering*). I have to. They heard me typing.

DAVID (*rubbing himself with his arms, as if cold*). Let's keep on
writing. Sonia. Damn. If I had permission for a computer . . . .

SONIA. Quiet!

> SONIA *crosses to the door, as* DAVID *sits at the typewriter.*
> *She opens halfway. She can see* DANIEL LUCAS, *but he*
> *cannot see her yet.*

DANIEL LUCAS (*shy*). David Malko?

SONIA (*suspicious*). He's not in. (*Pause.*)

DANIEL LUCAS. I'm – a publisher. A friend of Bergante's. He –
suggested this visit. (*Pause.*) I've read the novel.

> SONIA *hesitates, then opens.* DANIEL LUCAS *is astonished*
> *to see someone who so resembles* TANIA.

SONIA. Please come in. I'm Mrs. Malko – but you can call me
Sonia.

> DANIEL LUCAS *doesn't move.*

SONIA. Is there something wrong?

> DANIEL LUCAS *leans against the door, as if he were about to*
> *faint.*

DANIEL LUCAS (*weakly*). Nothing. It's – a dizzy spell, I get
them some – For a moment, I thought – I thought –
(*Recovering.*) A mere coincidence. Meaningless as dreams.

SONIA (*turns, entering the room*). Love, this gentleman . . .
Mr . . . . Mr . . . .

> DANIEL LUCAS *comes into the austere, cold room. Lights*
> *rise and we see that* DAVID MALKO *is played by the same*
> *actor who plays* NICK *and* ENRIQUE, *but he has glasses on.*
> DAVID *sits at the typewriter. He unwraps his arms, begins to*

type furiously. DANIEL LUCAS *is stunned at this second resemblance, falls into a chair.*

SONIA. He's a publisher. A friend of Bergante's – But he's – I'm afraid you really are not well, sir. (*Pause.*) Maybe a cup of coffee would do you –

DANIEL LUCAS. It's nothing, I'll be – I'll be . . . This is the house of – You are – David Malko?

DAVID *gets up from the machine, shakes* DANIEL*'s hand.*

DAVID. Who else would I be? Unemployed, working with my merciless characters – Malko Incorporated. Hey – you look as if you'd seen a ghost.

SONIA. David!

DAVID. Well, he does.

SONIA. Our – guest has read 'Turns', David.

DAVID. Well, he's going to be the only one –

SONIA. There you go again – always so negative. If you want to be successful, write something different, but don't complain all day long –

DAVID (*to* DANIEL LUCAS). Didn't Bergante say it was hopeless? Isn't that what that guy called the Pope said?

DANIEL LUCAS (*beginning to recover*). The – Pope?

DAVID. 'Cause he's infallible, they say.

DANIEL LUCAS. And Bergante gave you no other details about this – ?

DAVID. Only that everybody calls him the Pope. And that it was hopeless.

SONIA *sits down behind* DAVID, *looks fixedly at* DANIEL LUCAS.

DANIEL LUCAS. You give up hope too easily, Mr. – Malko. Your characters would never accept defeat so –

DAVID. Yeah, but they're fiction.

DANIEL LUCAS. But quite – well life-like, wouldn't you say? I mean, your characters – this – Don Alfonso, ah, Morales I think it is, he must be modelled on someone real, someone must have told you about –

DAVID. Well, I'm glad someone thinks the son of a bitch is life-like. I think he's pretty lifeless, if you want my opinion, but he's not modelled on –

DANIEL LUCAS. That woman then, she –

DAVID. What woman?

DANIEL LUCAS. The mother, Tanya, the one who returns, that one –

DAVID. This guy doesn't read very closely, does he? The mother's not called – Tanya. She hasn't got a name. Dead people don't have names.

DANIEL LUCAS. So she's dead? She is dead, that woman, isn't – ?

DAVID. Hey, did you read – See, Sonia, they don't understand a fuck – that's what happens when the only ones who get to read you are censors –

DANIEL LUCAS. What censors?

DAVID. Bastards! Fifty years controlling every adjective in the universe with the pretext of saving us from plagues they made themselves.

DANIEL LUCAS. You young people – you don't understand, do you, what things were like before our parents instituted these restrictions on – democratically instituted –

DAVID. Democratically – so most of the people are idiots, most of the people want to get screwed, does that – ?

DANIEL LUCAS. Idiots? The idiots were the ones who would not accept sacrifices to stop the plague, to secure the streets, secure our bodies. I've studied what it was like: the moaning naked women plastered on every screen, the children saturated with sex and violence and vulgarity, the poor incited to aggression and despair by wild savage music, the lack of tradition and discipline corroding the very fabric of –

DAVID (*stands up, agitated*). Bullshit! Bullshit publicity. I'm surprised a friend of Bergante's would swallow such – Hey, why did old Bergante send you anyway?

SONIA. You must forgive my husband, sir. He's –

DAVID. Answer the question or get the fuck out!

DANIEL LUCAS. Bergante wants to know – when your novel will be finished. And he asked about the ending, also about the ending.

DAVID. He wants a happy ending, huh?

DANIEL LUCAS. We all want a happy ending.

DAVID. Well too bad. Tell Bergante I'm not going to change a word to accommodate anyone. And if it takes a hundred years before my work gets green-lighted, then it'll –

DANIEL LUCAS (*barely controlling himself*). Mr. Malko – let me say that you would do well to learn some humbleness from your lifeless characters. Let me say no more. Though yes, yes. Accommodation to the messy world around you: An authorisation for a computer, for a preproduction budget, for a reading with actors, a contract, none of this would hurt you, would it?

DANIEL LUCAS *stands in front of* DAVID, *who is seated, both of them exactly in the same position as the* DIRECTOR *and* DANIEL LUCAS *in a previous scene.*

DAVID. Hey, are you offering me a job?

DANIEL LUCAS. No, of course not, I'm just –

DAVID. Trying to bribe me? Trying to get me to stop writing?

DANIEL LUCAS. Not at all. But if you were to change your text slightly, diminish your disaparagement of what ordinary people believe – a few dialogues snipped delicately here, the softening of an idea there and –

DAVID. Not one snip, not one snap. That's how you start, and soon you start rewriting whole chunks –

DANIEL LUCAS. I don't see what difference a few words could –

DAVID. A few words? You know what, Sonia? This guy's a fucking ecofascist. The hell to him and to Bergante and while I'm at it, the hell to that Pope guy too. Fuck the lot of you! C'mon, honey, let's get some work done.

SONIA. David! Control yourself.

DAVID. C'mon, Sonia – it's the mother/son scene. When they finally meet in prison. Maybe this guy will get bored and he'll leave.

DANIEL LUCAS (*to himself, alarmed*). They can't meet. She's dead. The mother can't –

As DAVID *types,* SONIA *reads over his shoulder.*

SONIA. So she says: Do you know who I am?

DAVID. And so far we have Enrique saying: I've seen you before.

SONIA. But not in photographs.

DAVID. Not in photographs. Hmm. That doesn't sound quite right. I mean – they're both tied to chairs, right? And he's – hardly able to breathe, so . . .

DANIEL LUCAS (*muttering, to himself*). Oh, my God!

SONIA. What if he were to answer: No, my dad burnt all your photographs.

DAVID (*typing*). Right. My dad burnt all your photographs. But I saw you in my dreams.

DANIEL *watches* DAVID *and* SONIA *become* NICK *and* TANYA.

SONIA. And in those dreams did I tell you what happened to me?

DAVID. All I know is that you – came to our house that day.

SONIA. I was inside when your father arrived. I was combing my hair.

DANIEL LUCAS (*anguished*). Enough, enough! I have to go, I have to go.

DANIEL LUCAS *stands, hastily, goes to the door.* SONIA *follows him outside. Lights go down on* DAVID *inside.*

SONIA. I'm sorry. We've been rude.

DANIEL LUCAS. So there's – no way of saving the boy?

SONIA. It depends on what you call saving – but there are ways.

DANIEL LUCAS. How?

SONIA. Read the novel when it comes out. Or see the movie.

DANIEL LUCAS. And if I have to wait, as your husband suggested, a hundred years?

SONIA (*suddenly, as if she had recognised him*). That depends on you.

DANIEL LUCAS. I must be – It's getting late.

SONIA. I wish you the best of luck, sir. You and your family. I hope things go well for you.

DANIEL LUCAS. I thank you for your consideration, madame, but there is no reason to believe that –

SONIA. I'm only saying it because today – I noticed that today you came without your umbrella.

DANIEL LUCAS. I do not use an umbrella, madame.

SONIA. Perhaps I confused you, sir, with someone else.

DANIEL LUCAS. Perhaps. These things do happen – confusions of this sort, I mean.

SONIA. You can trust me.

She waits. He hesitates.

DANIEL LUCAS. Many years ago . . . I – I – made – I think I made a mistake, many years ago.

SONIA. Some mistakes are not – irreparable.

DANIEL LUCAS. And some are.

SONIA. There is a saying in the town where I was born. To drive
    out a nail –

DANIEL LUCAS. You need another nail. Yes. A long time ago
    someone – she was just like you – used to say things like that.

SONIA. Did she ever tell you not to be afraid?

DANIEL LUCAS. Too many times.

SONIA. We can never say that too many times.

DANIEL LUCAS. She said it too many times. I grew to – fear her.

SONIA. I am sorry to hear that. (*Pause.*) Take care of yourself.
    And your son.

SONIA *exits. Down the street,* DANIEL LUCAS *sees the*
    MAN, *waiting and watching.*

MAN. Looking for somebody?

DANIEL LUCAS. No, I –

MAN. Because I am. I am looking for somebody. If you know
    what I mean. I'm looking for anybody who wants to fuck with
    the borders. So don't. That's where meaning starts: knowing
    what the limit is. That's the one thing a father can teach his son.
    So why don't you – go home. To your son. If you have a home,
    that is. And if you still have a son.

DANIEL LUCAS. I'm warning you. Leave my boy alone.

MAN. I was never a boy. Were you ever a boy?

DANIEL LUCAS. What do you mean?

MAN. I don't remember ever having been a boy. In my profession,
    you don't need a childhood. Of course, there are some boys
    who never grow up. They just stay that way – forever. If you
    know what I mean?

DANIEL LUCAS. Who are you?

MAN. Maybe I'm your friend. Maybe I'm the only friend you've
    ever had. Think about it.

The MAN *exits.* DANIEL LUCAS *is desperate. He takes out
    his cellular phone. He dials a number.*

DANIEL LUCAS. Maybe there's still time.

Lights rise on the anteroom where IRENE *answers the phone.*

IRENE. Mr. Lucas – where have you been? The Director's been calling all morning about –

DANIEL LUCAS. Never mind him. Enrique, did he – ?

IRENE. Who?

DANIEL LUCAS. My son Nick, Nick, did he call to –

IRENE. The one who's been calling like crazy is the Director. He's asking about the signature.

DANIEL LUCAS. I'll get it for him. Just find Nick.

IRENE. Nick's here, in your office.

DANIEL LUCAS. Keep him there. Do you understand?

IRENE. I don't understand a thing, but I'll keep him here, sure.

The lights rise on DANIEL LUCAS*'s office,* NICK *waiting inside.* DANIEL LUCAS *crosses the stage and enters the anteroom.*

IRENE. Oh, God, I'm glad you –

DANIEL LUCAS. Where's Nick? Have they come for him? Have they?

IRENE. He's in there. Get a hold of yourself.

DANIEL LUCAS. Myself?

IRENE. Where have you been?

DANIEL LUCAS. At Malko's.

IRENE. So you saw him? What did he – ?

DANIEL LUCAS. I don't know if I saw him.

IRENE. Malko? How can't you not know ?

DANIEL LUCAS. It was as if I was – I was – visiting, listen, Jacqueline –

IRENE. Jacqueline?

DANIEL. . . . as if I was visiting my own self, the man I – Quick. The book. Give it to me. I'll find out what the limping bastard is going to do –

IRENE. What limping bastard?

DANIEL LUCAS. Alfonso Morales.

IRENE. Problem is: I sent it back to Bergante this morning.

DANIEL LUCAS. But I haven't reached the part where – I need to read what they're planning – if they hunt down his son, if Nick is – that's how I'll know what –

IRENE. I told Bergante that story was – cursed, that it was affecting your – well, I didn't say your – performance, I just told him I was getting it the hell out of here.

DANIEL LUCAS. They're after him, Irene.

DANIEL LUCAS *goes into his office.*

Thank God, Nick, I thought they might have already –

NICK (*cold, angry*). I know everything.

DANIEL LUCAS. What do you know?

NICK. About Mom.

DANIEL LUCAS. There's nothing to – listen, Nick, what matters now is to save you, to make sure that –

NICK. I have proof.

DANIEL LUCAS. We don't have time for – If we don't keep the Director on our side, they'll – Nick, they'll –

Sound of a typewriter. Dimly lit view of DAVID MALKO's house, shadows of DAVID and SONIA. Lights on DANIEL and NICK begin to change, grow murky and swirling, enveloping DANIEL LUCAS and NICK.

NICK. They'll what – ?

DANIEL LUCAS (*as the typewriter continues*). They'll – they'll –

NICK (*reminding us more and more of ENRIQUE*). They'll what – what they did to my mother?

Lights go up on SONIA in the house, seated at the typewriter. DAVID's silhouette is behind her, barely discernible.

DANIEL LUCAS. Nobody did anything to your mother. Who has been spreading stories about – ?

NICK/ENRIQUE. I wish they were stories. But Mom died in a Readjustment Centre.

DANIEL LUCAS. That's a lie. Your mother died in our house. I was with her when she –

NICK/ENRIQUE. I know what happened, Dad. Somebody – told me.

DANIEL LUCAS. Nothing happened.

NICK/ENRIQUE. Why did you send her there, Dad? What did you fear?

DANIEL LUCAS (*hesitantly*). Nothing.

The sound of the typewriter stops and the lights on the MALKO *house fade. Only a ghostly beam on* SONIA *is left. She lets her hair loose and becomes* TANYA.

TANYA. There's only one way out. 'Love consists of this/ A dialogue of solitudes.'

NICK/ENRIQUE. You betrayed her, didn't you?

DANIEL LUCAS (*overlapping*). No, no, no.

NICK/ENRIQUE. Yes, you signed her name, you gagged her, you sent for the Director . . .

DANIEL LUCAS. No, no.

NICK/ENRIQUE. Yes, you watched them take her away. Didn't you? Didn't you?

DANIEL LUCAS. Yes. Yes. Yes. Damn you.

TANYA *disappears.*

NICK/ENRIQUE. Damn you. What happened to her? Did you kill her?

DANIEL LUCAS *sags in a chair, holding his head in his hands.*

DANIEL LUCAS. After that day, I never saw her again. I never knew what they did to her. I never tried to find out. Years later I heard she died. That afternoon you came back and then we went out for an ice-cream. You liked vanilla . . . Say something . . . Don't look at me like that. I wasn't the only one. Everybody was – Back then – you don't understand – back then everybody did it. It was that or accomplish nothing, watch your life go by in smoke, waste away your life eternally on the outside, and she just wouldn't play along, she was just – she was so stubborn. Don't you understand? I was afraid. We were all afraid. I believed in a cause.

The DIRECTOR *enters the anteroom, shushes* IRENE, *begins to listen outside the door.*

DANIEL LUCAS. Please say something. Anything. Nick?

NICK/ENRIQUE. You limping bastard.

DANIEL LUCAS. I wanted to save you pain.

NICK/ENRIQUE. If you wanted to save me pain, you should have killed me when I came home that day.

The DIRECTOR *and* IRENE *enter the office. The lights change and become normal again.*

DIRECTOR. Good morrow and good morning or would it be more appropriate to wish you a good afternoon, Mr. Danny Luke.

IRENE. It's 11:56, Director. Not afternoon yet.

DIRECTOR. Well, well, Irene. Learning from the master to be mathematical. And here's our young friend Nicholas, ready for action – Ready to find some lucky girl, some lucky computer, ready to be one of the multitude of happy couples honouring Our Fifty Years of Moral Resources. (*Pause.*) So . . . ?

DANIEL LUCAS. I'll be back right away, sir.

DANIEL LUCAS *exits to the anteroom with* IRENE, *leaving* NICK *with the* DIRECTOR. DANIEL LUCAS *signs a piece of paper.*

DANIEL LUCAS (*whispering*). Ni-cho-las Lu-cas. There he finally is.

IRENE. You can't do that, Daniel.

DANIEL LUCAS. I've got to save the boy. Everything I've done I did for him, so he could be safe – Now I –

DANIEL LUCAS *goes into his office, hands paper to the* DIRECTOR.

DANIEL LUCAS. High-noon, sir. The Lucas family quota.

DIRECTOR. Good for the Lucas family. I knew I could count on you. And on this boy. My congratulations, young man. Just one thing, I'm just asking for one thing. I want the first one. The first kid is mine to name and baptize and celebrate. The first – is mine.

The DIRECTOR *exults, takes out some cigars, passes them around. The chimes of the Smiley Minute begin to sound. Everybody but* NICK *automatically smiles.* DANIEL LUCAS *gives* IRENE *a hug, the* DIRECTOR *turns to* NICK *to embrace him.* NICK *takes a step backward.*

NICK. That's not my signature.

Nobody moves. Only the sound of the chimes continue for several beats, and then die out.

DANIEL LUCAS. That's Nick for you. Can't help making last minute jokes –

NICK. He forged my signature.

DIRECTOR. But why should a loyal young man like you need anybody to forge anything on his behalf, not when marriage is such a sacred sacrament –

NICK. Don't speak to me about the sacredness of marriage, you
hypocrite. I know what you did to my mother. Is she alive? Or
did you have her killed?

DIRECTOR. The accusations seem to have a way of
accumulating, don't they? For a loyal young man –

NICK. I'm not a loyal young man.

DANIEL LUCAS. Nick!

NICK. Don't even try and protect me, you old son of a bitch.

IRENE. Nick, how dare you speak to your –

NICK. Stay out of this.

IRENE. I'm in it because –

NICK. Because the old bastard is fucking you.

IRENE. No. He's not . . .

NICK. Then he's a fool as well as a liar.

IRENE. You don't get it, do you? Your father's going to lose his
job because of –

DIRECTOR. Oh, no, no, Irene, that's where you're wrong. We're
giving our friend Luke here my post.

NICK. For forging my signature, you're –

DIRECTOR. Here is a man so loyal to Moral Resources that he's
ready to use fraud to get his rebellious only son to commit to
our Company's happy marriage policy. It was a test, Luke –
and you passed with flying colours. And we were also testing,
well, your family – right? Because we've been suspecting this
little Nicholas for a long time – and now it's out in the open:
you've been a member of the free love conspiracy all these
years. We just needed someone to help us flush the damn traitor
from our midst – and that has been your stellar role, Daniel
Lucas – and the reward is – a promotion.

DANIEL LUCAS. I – I'm grateful, sir, of course – and would be
even more if you could see fit to show some mercy towards my
– After all, it's only one case, only this one –

DIRECTOR. I'm surprised, Daniel. As the new Director, surely
you know the value of – symbols, representations, metaphors,
examples.

DANIEL LUCAS. But he's – sorry, sir, he's – Aren't you, Nick?

NICK *does not say a word.*

DIRECTOR. Nick is not cooperating. (*Picking up the phone.*) Yes,
we've got him. Confession and all. It worked beautifully. I'll be

down with him right away. (*He hangs up.*) Or would you rather they come up and drag you down the stairs?

DANIEL LUCAS. Nick. Please . . .

DIRECTOR. I think you should come and visit him later – when he's in a more cooperative mood. Twenty-four hours, let's say forty-eight, Daniel.

DANIEL LUCAS. Please – don't hurt the boy, don't –

DIRECTOR. Not all pain is bad, Daniel. Some pain is – well, good for you. Hmmm. Where did I hear that? Or is it something I read? But then – you would be the first to agree, as new Director, sir, that you shouldn't believe everything you read.

The DIRECTOR *begins to exit with* NICK *in custody.*

DANIEL LUCAS. Isn't there – ? Isn't there anything – I can do?

DIRECTOR (*smiling*). Maybe it's time you killed – Alfonso Morales.

DIRECTOR *and* NICK *exit.* DANIEL *and* IRENE *look at each other.*

IRENE. What does he mean?

DANIEL LUCAS. He read that book. How could he have – ? But he trapped us by using that twisted, perverted piece of trash. Everything in it has come true so far – everything –

IRENE. Everything? So what he said about your – wife . . . ?

DANIEL LUCAS. Irene – I – we shouldn't talk about this – now is not the –

IRENE. 'All these years, he did not trust Jacqueline with his secrets.' Is that also true? That you don't love me?

DANIEL LUCAS. No, of course, I –

IRENE. 'Love consists in this/ That two solitudes protect/'

DANIEL LUCAS. 'And touch and greet each other.'

IRENE. You said that to your wife. And then you betrayed her. How can I be sure you won't betray me?

DANIEL LUCAS. Damn lies. Damn lies in that damn book. Bring me form 492.

IRENE. Form 492?

DANIEL LUCAS. Denies the author access to any possible publication, production, contract – till the day he dies. Forever. Jails him if he writes one more word.

IRENE. That's your answer? To ban the book? To forbid the author forever? Because he's writing the truth about you? That's your way of proving you love me?

DANIEL LUCAS. That's the way I'll prove that Malko's damn book hasn't got any power over me: so it will never come true. I'm being tested, Jacqueline, tested. My son is in danger, you don't believe me any more, somebody knows everything about me – I've got to kill Alfonso Morales.

The sound of a typewriter, Lights rise on DAVID MALKO typing. SONIA looks over his shoulder. Murky, swirling lights on DANIEL and IRENE as they gradually become DON ALFONSO and JACQUELINE.

IRENE. And what if you were to – what if you were to release the book? What if that is the real test? Release it so everybody will know your story, know you are willing to change, prove you will never betray someone like me ever again? You have the power to do it – you're the Director now. They can't know it's released until it's too late. Alfonso? Are you listening to me?

DON ALFONSO *limps towards her, agitated, moves in the direction of the typewriter, comes back, stops, scratches his head.*

DON ALFONSO. I can release it without their knowing, yes, but then what? Once it's out there, do you know what they'll do to me, to Enrique? Do you know what they'll do to you?

DAVID (*in front of the typewriter*). Okay. We've got Don Alfonso Morales scratching his head. He's ready to kill. He looks at her, he says (*Typing.*) This damn story is eating my mind up.

DON ALFONSO (*scratching his head*). It's eating my mind up. I've got to get rid of it.

SONIA. So what if she says: Alfonso. But you can't.

JACQUELINE. But you can't.

DAVID (*typing*). But you can't. You can't betray your dignity. No, that's too sentimental. Too obvious. You can't betray your –

SONIA. Son?

DAVID. That will come later. Maybe just keep it like that, not give it away so soon. You can't betray your – betray your –

JACQUELINE. You can't betray your – betray your –

DON ALFONSO. The person I once wanted to be? Is that what you're saying, that I can't betray the person I once wanted to be?

DAVID. I've got it. The person I once – once wanted to be. That's what Don Alfonso answers.

SONIA. Then Jacqueline says: Whatever your decision, just remember you have to live with it from now on.

DAVID (*typing*) . . . . remember you have to live with it from now on.

DON ALFONSO. Yes. Live with it from now on.

JACQUELINE. Forever. Just like you have to live with what you did to her.

DON ALFONSO. But if I release it, if I . . . if I . . . .

There is a long moment of silence.

DIRECTOR's VOICE (*from the darkness*). What did he say? (*Silence*). Did I hear him say: But if I release it, if I . . . If I . . . What does that mean? (*Silence.*) David? What does it mean?

The lights rise on the DIRECTOR. *He is seated in a chair, marked* DIRECTOR.

DAVID (*turning to him*). I – I don't know.

The DIRECTOR *walks over to* DAVID.

DIRECTOR. I don't know, sir.

DAVID. I don't know, sir.

DIRECTOR. We don't believe you. Somebody in your fucking story does something, then somebody in fucking reality does the exact same thing, over and over, – and vice-versa, like germs crisscrossing borders as if they were water, and you tell us that one thing's unrelated to the other – so you explain to me how I can be sure that my friend Danny Lucas is not going to end up like Alfonso Morales – wondering if he should betray me.

DAVID. It's – it was just fiction, sir. A – metaphor.

DIRECTOR. But I didn't write it. Did I write it? So you tell me. What happens next?

The DIRECTOR *reads from the typewriter.*

DIRECTOR. He asks: Have you thought of the consequences? Good question. And our Jacqueline answers . . . Let's see: That he should deal with the consequences later.

JACQUELINE. We'll deal with the consequences later.

DIRECTOR. And that's as far as it goes. Not another word. Blank page. Waiting to be written. So – what do we do now?

DAVID. Were you asking – me, sir?

DIRECTOR. Who else could I be asking? What happens next?

The DIRECTOR *comes up behind* DAVID, *strips him of his upper layers of clothing, leaving him naked from the waist up.* DAVID *shivers, rubs himself with his arms and hands.*

DIRECTOR. I'll tell you what we're going to do. We're going to write something – together. A little, little collaboration. Have our Don Alfonso ban the book.

DAVID. Sir?

DIRECTOR. Have him ban it. Write it down. Don Alfonso bans the damn book where Daniel Lucas is a character.

SONIA. I don't think we can – write that.

DIRECTOR. Oh, you'll write it.

The DIRECTOR *brings* SONIA *to* DAVID's *side.*

DIRECTOR. In your story, David, you allow Enrique to heroically suffer during his interrogation, but you didn't put him to the ultimate test. Because what's really intolerable, David, is pain done to others. Your mother, your sweetheart, your wife. Anything female will finally do. Anything that can give birth will do.

SONIA. Don't do it.

DAVID. Sonia!

SONIA. Don't let them do this to us, David.

The DIRECTOR *sits* SONIA *in a chair, gags her.*

DIRECTOR. Everything human eventually cooperates.

A moment of silence.

DON ALFONSO. Wait!

There is a long silence. They all look at him. DON ALFONSO *stands up and, leaning on his umbrella, limps towards the edge of the light separating him from* DAVID, SONIA *and the* DIRECTOR.

DON ALFONSO. Ask me! Ask me what happens next.

MAN'S VOICE *(harsh, from the darkness).* What did he say?

DON ALFONSO. I said to ask me. Leave her alone. I'm the one who knows.

MAN'S VOICE *(from the darkness).* Did he say that he's the one who knows?

DON ALFONSO. Yes. I'm the one who decides what happens next.

DIRECTOR. Well, well. Look who's finally decided to speak for himself.

DON ALFONSO *takes another step forward. Lights rise on the* MAN.

MAN (*casual, friendly*). If I were you, my man, I'd stop right there.

DON ALFONSO *stops on the edge.*

Didn't I tell you not to fuck with the borders? Isn't that the one piece of friendly advice I've been giving you?

DIRECTOR. I think you should listen to him.

MAN. If I were you, I'd just go back to being who I was, that's what I'd do. Because once you cross the border, once you break down the barriers, step across the line, if you know what I mean – then it's a one-way ticket. There's no going back. It's like – like death. Or like birth, if you want to be more positive, I suppose.

DIRECTOR (*laughing*). It's not too late, Alfonso. Just go back and leave things to me. Like we did in the past.

DON ALFONSO. You son of a bitch, you've been setting me up, testing me, feeding information to my son, playing with me all this time, fucking with me –

DIRECTOR. Hold it, Alfonso – or maybe I should call you, Daniel, but let's stick with Alfonso for now, shall we? Let's get things straight. I am not the one playing with you. Or fucking with you. This man and his wife are playing with you. Your son has been playing with you. Your lover is playing with you. And fucking you. Not me. They were the ones manipulating you, trying to confuse you, melt the borders of your identity, drive you insane so you would release their subversive, contagious story into the world. Not me. I'm being set up as the villain of this story – when in fact all along I've been the only one looking out for your interests. As I promised the day I came to visit you, the day I came to offer you this job. And now I'm going to keep my promise.

DON ALFONSO. What are you going to do?

DIRECTOR. Let me ask you something. If you had to choose between possessing a man's body and posssessing his soul, what would you choose?

DON ALFONSO. That's – that's not a question I like.

DIRECTOR. Uncertainty is never good for us, my Pope, my Old
Eagle Eyes. A blank page! Yes. A blank page is like an
undiscovered country – waiting to be filled up, waiting to be
written. All within neat patrolled borders. I'm going to fill up
the blank page in your life. I'm going to give this story the right
ending. (*To* DAVID MALKO.) Alfonso Morales bans the damn
book. Or Daniel Lucas bans the damn story. Does it matter who
bans it, as long as somebody does it, here, now, later,
somewhere, sometime?

MAN. It seems he doesn't want to cooperate.

DIRECTOR. Remember Tanya?

The DIRECTOR *takes* DAVID*'s hand and puts it on* SONIA*'s
breast.*

DIRECTOR. What's that called? (*Pause.*) Definitely not a bosom.
(*Pause.*) This man bans the book. You write it or she writes it.
Just a few words. Come on. A few words.

DAVID *types a few words on the typewriter.*

DAVID (*haltingly*). Our hero bans the story.

Almost like an automaton, DON ALFONSO *takes the form
from* JACQUELINE, *sits at his desk.*

DIRECTOR. Right. So now everything's back to normal.

MAN (*gesturing to* DAVID *and* SONIA). How about these two?

DIRECTOR. Well, it doesn't really matter any more. I mean,
they've got nothing more to say, have they? Not one snip, not
one snap, huh, David? Where's your arrogance now, David
Malko, famous author?

The DIRECTOR *makes a gesture. Blackout on* DAVID
MALKO*'s house. A long silence. He makes the lights come on
again.* DAVID *and* SONIA *have disappeared.*

DIRECTOR. You want to know what happened? Maybe we
offered our unknown author a job, maybe he's snipping and
snapping in some office right now, maybe he'll be starring in
his own show in a couple of decades from now – or maybe,
well, something else happened, and we don't need to know
what – the guidelines say no violence, they say no blood. Quiet
and discreet. As long as we don't hear from them again. Now
for the good news. The boy is saved. Don Alfonso Morales has
saved his son! Or would we rather. . . . ?

DIRECTOR *makes a gesture like a magician. On another part
of the stage, a piercing beam of light falls on* ENRIQUE, *who
twists and screams silently, as if on a rack. The* DIRECTOR

*makes another gesture with his hands and the lights black out
and come on – and* ENRIQUE *is bathed in a soft colourful
light, in perfect health.*

ENRIQUE (*cheerful*). Thanks, Dad. They're letting me go. They're
fixing everything. Forgetting, erasing everything I said –

DIRECTOR. Rewrites! Rewrites! Forgetting, erasing everything
he said, anything you said. Back we go. We get rid of all that
melodramatic junk. I mean, who wants to hear him say:

ENRIQUE. If you wanted to save me pain, you should have killed
me when I came home that day.

DIRECTOR. Melodramatic. Doesn't make the cut. Those lines end
up on the cutting-room floor. Gone. In fact, we're getting rid of
that whole scene – definitely not a family value. So when you,
my friend, told your son: 'I held her hand while she died.' What
he answers is :

ENRIQUE. That must have been hard, Dad. But – we made it.
You've been like a mother to me.

DIRECTOR. That's it. We don't want uncomfortable readers or
audiences or sponsors. So make things easy for all of us, my
friend. All dynasties start with a murder. Somebody's going to
die and if it's not – I already told you: it's time to kill Daniel
Lucas. Ban that futuristic novel whose hero is just like you,
except he doesn't limp. Come on, Alfonso: sign the fucking
form.

DON ALFONSO *signs the form.*

And now there's only one finishing touch, an inspiring finale
that ties everything neatly together with – let's see – with this
lovely piece of a woman, this pretty baby, we've left you out in
the cold all this while. Let's have some romantic music, something that'll move the audience to tears – come on, come on –
(Romantic strings waft through the air.) A surprise ending. Our
boy here and our girl here are going to marry. The computer's
found that they are just right for each other. Keep each other out
of trouble.

The DIRECTOR *frantically stages the scene, dragging*
ENRIQUE *to* JACQUELINE's *side, setting up a take, getting
rid of office furniture.*

Our hero never really loved her anyway, but to make sure the
audience is not upset at this – turn of events, he gives her up,
blesses the happy young couple. C'mon, c'mon. We're rolling
here. I want a light on this man.

A dim light comes on ALFONSO.

When I say a light, I mean a real light. For a real man, father, player. Not a wimpy, wavering light. A killer of a light.

The DIRECTOR *raises his arms like a magician and strong lights illuminate* ALFONSO.

There! Bless you, my children. C'mon. Let's hear it. Bless you my children. Alfonso!

DON ALFONSO (*with difficulty*). Bless you, my – children.

DIRECTOR. Hey, you two, let's show some passion. Only two seconds though. And no body contact, erections, now, we want to keep this chaste, keep it subtle. What if you place your hand discreetly on her womb, huh? Hope the public realises that your first grandchild is on its way. And if they begin to feel that you are stranded, left alone – why, another surprise turn – We'll bring Tanya back – or whatever she's called – from the insane asylum or from the dead or wherever she is – bring her back repentant, part of our collective happy wedding ceremony in our new Moral Resources stadium.

DON ALFONSO. Please, sir . . . .

DIRECTOR. Cut. Cut. Is that line in the script? Did I write that motherfucker? You – quiet – I want no noise while this scene is being – I'm surprised you're not – well, happy, Alf, my boy. I'm only doing what you've been doing all these years to other people's work. And I didn't hear anyone objecting then. As a matter of fact, I don't hear any objection now either. (*To the audience.*) Do I? Do I see anybody out there who's willing to risk everything for an illusion, a delusion, a fucking metaphor? Anybody who's so hot for heroes, eager for redemption, that they're ready to break out of – or break into – their little little lives? Good. No objections. Now, where were we? Ah yes. What seems to be missing is our heroine. Some words of endearment? (JACQUELINE *says nothing.*) Well, our lady love here is embarrassed and I can't say I blame her. But blushing acceptance simply isn't enough. We need your voice, darling: Alfonso, thank you for being such a man about this. Jacqueline? Alfonso, thank you for being –

JACQUELINE. Alfonso, it doesn't have to be like this.

DIRECTOR. Wrong lines, honey.

JACQUELINE. Alfonso, if they can rewrite you, you can rewrite them. Don't let them do this to us.

DIRECTOR. Don't flub your lines, woman.

JACQUELINE (*angry*). I'm not flubbing anything. These are my own lines.

DIRECTOR *sidles up to* JACQUELINE. *She avoids him.*

DIRECTOR. Look who's suddenly full of literary pretensions.

JACQUELINE. Yes, look who's suddenly speaking. Nobody
expects it of me and it's not in anybody's novel or script but
I also have a story to tell. Once in a while the little little people
do have stories to tell. Even the people who get their asses
pinched in the hallways, even we have something to say,
especially if it's about where we end up.

DIRECTOR. So you want a different ending? Why didn't you say
so? I could accommodate you quite pleasurably.

DIRECTOR *fondles* JACQUELINE. *She sends him sprawling.*

JACQUELINE. How about an ending in which I screw you,
Director, instead of an ending in which you screw me and
everybody else? An ending in which all these years I've been
copying your secret files, an ending in which I show your wife
and your lover and the press the photos of the little girls you've
pawed, the secretaries you fucked under this desk, the cunts
you've forced open with a broomstick, the lives you've ruined,
the massacres you've covered up, the forests you've destroyed.
All in the name of morality and God.

DIRECTOR. You wanted a different ending, you bitch – you've
got it. (*To the* MAN.) You know what to do to her.

MAN. Why me?

DIRECTOR. She broke the rules, didn't she? Crossed the line?
Didn't she?

The MAN *grabs* JACQUELINE, *forces her into a chair, gags
and ties her, drags the chair off into the darkness.*

DIRECTOR. These women, my God. Tanya, Sonia, Jacqueline,
Irene. It's like a fucking merry-go-round . . . . As for you.

DON ALFONSO. Yes. I am here. You can always count on me.

DIRECTOR. You know what I want.

DON ALFONSO. You want me to write her confession. And sign
it with her name.

DIRECTOR. Just like you did with Tanya, yes.

DON ALFONSO. Right. And tomorrow you'll ask me to do it
again, right? Again and again and again. Until the day I die?
Right? Because this is who I am. This is what I write. This is
the life I wrote for myself.

DIRECTOR. This is the life you wrote for yourself. Sign her name
and be done with it. You never loved her anyway.

DON ALFONSO *limps across the stage to the typewriter. He sits down in front of it.*

DIRECTOR. Good boy.

DON ALFONSO *begins to type. Then he stops.*

DON ALFONSO. Director. I would like – would you answer something?

DIRECTOR. A riddle. I love riddles.

DON ALFONSO *types some more.*

DON ALFONSO. How do you recognise somebody, Director? If you had to choose one thing that – just one thing that makes somebody who he is – what would it be?

DIRECTOR. I don't know what you're getting at.

DON ALFONSO *continues typing.*

DON ALFONSO. Let me put it another way: what do we leave behind when we die?

DIRECTOR. Let's see. Some people leave children.

DON ALFONSO. Children who hate us. What else?

DIRECTOR. Memories.

DON ALFONSO. The harm we did.

DON ALFONSO *types a few more words.*

DIRECTOR. God, you're in a negative mood. Think of all the good we do. Think of all the folks we've entertained. And now it's your turn: so tell me – what can I do for you? How can I cheer you up? I mean, we don't want our new Director depressing everybody's Smiley Minutes.

DON ALFONSO. I want to see her.

DIRECTOR. You're a cruel man, Alfonso. You want to mock her? Or fuck her? Or both?

DON ALFONSO. I want to see her.

DIRECTOR. As long as you're finished with that.

DON ALFONSO *taps one more word, takes the piece of paper out of the typewriter.* DIRECTOR *makes a gesture. A dim light rises on* JACQUELINE *on the other side of the stage, her torso tied to a chair, her eyes blindfolded.* DON ALFONSO *stands, picks up the umbrella, hesitates, then lets it fall. He crosses to her, not limping at all. For the first time,* DON ALFONSO *merges with* DANIEL LUCAS. *The stage is almost bare, a prison.* DANIEL/ALFONSO *squats down next to* IRENE/JACQUELINE. *The* DIRECTOR *settles down comfortably to watch from the chair just vacated by* DANIEL/ALFONSO, *who grabs* IRENE/JACQUELINE*'s hands and puts them on his face.*

DANIEL/ALFONSO. Do you know what this is?

IRENE/JACQUELINE. Your face.

DANIEL/ALFONSO. No. It's my skull. If I were dead, in the dark, you wouldn't recognise it.

IRENE/JACQUELINE. I'd recognise you.

DANIEL/ALFONSO. Poor child. Out of love you say that, but if my skull lay next to – another man's skull on a dead table, you wouldn't know the difference. Underneath this skin, under this false face – no true self, only unrecognisable bones under the darkness. No, that's not how we recognise each other, that's not the way people should remember each other.

IRENE/JACQUELINE. You haven't come to save me, have you?

DANIEL/ALFONSO. I can't. I can't save anybody any more.

IRENE/JACQUELINE. So you've come to say good-bye?

DANIEL/ALFONSO. Yes.

DANIEL/ALFONSO *takes off her blindfold. They look at each other for a few beats. Then she disappears into the darkness.*

DIRECTOR. Well, that was a weird good-bye. Now what?

DANIEL/ALFONSO. Now I want to see my son.

DIRECTOR. Not before you sign. Then we'll release him.

DANIEL/ALFONSO. I want to see him now. I want him to understand why I am doing what I am doing.

DIRECTOR. In that case, your word is my command.

A light rises on NICK/ENRIQUE *tied to a chair.*

DANIEL/ALFONSO. My boy? My boy?

NICK/ENRIQUE. Dad, I – if you've come for me to forgive you –

DANIEL/ALFONSO. Shhhh. Don't say anything, my boy. We don't have much time. I want to tell you something. Remember when you were a child and you woke at night and you wanted a story, remember how I would always leave the ending for the next night? Remember? Well – it's the next night now – and that's why I've come. It's time to end this story.

NICK/ENRIQUE. What story?

DANIEL/ALFONSO. You know what story. It's about a man who believed dreams are meaningless, who scratches his head with his hand, a man who limped at times and at times didn't. That story.

NICK/ENRIQUE. And you've – now you know how it ends?

DANIEL/ALFONSO. That's why I'm here. Because I know how it ends.

NICK/ENRIQUE. So you've read it. Till the end.

DANIEL/ALFONSO. I don't need to read it. Not any more.

NICK/ENRIQUE. I don't understand.

DANIEL/ALFONSO. In that story, there's a son – his name is – a son who – things don't go very well for him, I'm afraid. Or for his – father.

DIRECTOR. Wait a second. What is this? What the hell is going on here?

The DIRECTOR *crosses the stage, towards* DANIEL/ALFONSO *and* NICK/ENRIQUE.

DIRECTOR. If you're double-crossing me, you're going to die, motherfucker. You and your son. Give me that confession you just wrote.

DANIEL/ALFONSO. It's not a confession.

DIRECTOR. What is it?

DANIEL/ALFONSO. You'll find out soon enough.

DIRECTOR. You can't do this.

DANIEL/ALFONSO. You can't stop me.

DIRECTOR. We'll see about that.

The DIRECTOR *makes a gesture. We hear the sound of boots, sirens, dogs in the darkness: a terrifying sense of impending doom. The* MAN *appears in a flashing howling light.*

DIRECTOR. Get him. Get him before he –

MAN. You can't touch him.

DIRECTOR. What do you mean?

MAN. The rules are the rules. Anybody can tell their story one last time.

DIRECTOR. But he's – he's breaking down the barriers, he's – crossing the borders.

MAN. He can do that. As long as he's willing to face the consequences. That's what I'm here for. To make sure everybody faces the consequences, everybody plays by the rules.

DIRECTOR. You poor bastard. To think I was worried about your soul. I was fond of you, Alfonso Morales, Daniel Lucas, whatever the fuck your name is.

MAN. The body. That's all there is – one day there's a body. The next day, not even a body. But while he's the owner of his body, he can fucking well do what he pleases with it. Then it's our turn.

DANIEL/ALFONSO. When?

MAN. I told you I was your friend.

DANIEL/ALFONSO. When is it over?

MAN. Soon. Not much time left. Time to say good-bye. Not much more.

The MAN *and the* DIRECTOR *fade into the shadows on either side of the stage, but do not entirely disappear, a faint glow on their faces and bodies.*

NICK/ENRIQUE. All of this is in the book . . . This scene, this meeting, we – That means you . . . You released the book.

DANIEL/ALFONSO. Yes.

NICK/ENRIQUE. That's what is on this piece of paper?

DANIEL/ALFONSO. Yes.

NICK/ENRIQUE. That's what you wrote? That's how this story ends?

DANIEL/ALFONSO. That's how. Right now, as we speak, somebody is watching, somebody is hearing us, reading us. Right now. But there's something missing. Something that hasn't been written yet – Are you listening? I want you to add something. It's something your mother would have wanted me to – Can you do that? For me? For us? As a way of saying – good-bye.

NICK/ENRIQUE. I can try.

DANIEL/ALFONSO. It's something your mother would have liked whispered to her, written on her wall before she died. It's something that comes after the last page of that book. Do you remember the last page?

DANIEL/ALFONSO *unties* NICK/ENRIQUE. *Sounds of terror approaching. Sirens, dogs, metal bars clattering against iron bars, orders, whispers, curses. Nearer and nearer.*

NICK/ENRIQUE. I remember the last page. When those men start to –

DANIEL/ALFONSO. No. Don't. I don't want to know. Have you got something to write with?

NICK/ENRIQUE. Yes, Dad.

NICK/ENRIQUE stands up.

DANIEL/ALFONSO. Write this then. This would come after the words: He was finally one person.

NICK/ENRIQUE. After: He was finally one person.

DANIEL/ALFONSO. After the words: The End. That's when this comes.

NICK/ENRIQUE. After the words: The End. Yes.

DANIEL/ALFONSO. Hurry.

The sound of men in boots running towards the stage. The shadowy faces of the MAN and the DIRECTOR become brighter, their bodies visible.

DANIEL/ALFONSO. Every book needs an epilogue. Write this down:

As NICK/ENRIQUE starts to write on the wall, facing the audience, DANIEL/ALFONSO painstakingly speaks above the din of the boots coming towards them:

'Epilogue. Once upon a time . . . '

NICK/ENRIQUE (*writing*). 'Once upon a time . . . '

DANIEL/ALFONSO. 'Once upon a time there was a man who was afraid . . . '

As DANIEL/ALFONSO speaks and his son writes, the DIRECTOR and the MAN emerge from the shadows and advance upon them. Blackout.

End of play.

A Nick Hern Book

Reader first published in Great Britain in 1995
by Nick Hern Books Limited, 14 Larden Road, London W3 7ST,
in association with the Traverse Theatre, Edinburgh

Reader copyright © 1995 by Ariel Dorfman

Front cover picture by Kevin Low, reproduced with permission

Typeset by Country Setting, Woodchurch, Kent TN26 3TB
Printed by Cox and Wyman Ltd, Reading, Berks

ISBN 1-85459-298-X

A CIP catalogue record for this book is available from
the British Library